AF784667

CONTENTS

S. Hrg. 103–1052

INTERSTATE IDENTIFICATION INDEX: IS IT AN EFFECTIVE WEAPON IN THE WAR AGAINST VIOLENT CRIME? IS IT INTERSTATE, DOES IT IDENTIFY, AND IS IT AN INDEX?

HEARING

BEFORE THE

COMMITTEE ON GOVERNMENTAL AFFAIRS UNITED STATES SENATE

ONE HUNDRED THIRD CONGRESS

SECOND SESSION

DECEMBER 6, 1994

Printed for the use of the Committee on Governmental Affairs

U.S. GOVERNMENT PRINTING OFFICE

86–004 CC WASHINGTON : 1995

For sale by the U.S. Government Printing Office
Superintendent of Documents, Congressional Sales Office, Washington, DC 20402
ISBN 0-16-047548-1

COMMITTEE ON GOVERNMENTAL AFFAIRS

JOHN GLENN, Ohio, *Chairman*

SAM NUNN, Georgia
CARL LEVIN, Michigan
JIM SASSER, Tennessee
DAVID PRYOR, Arkansas
JOSEPH I. LIEBERMAN, Connecticut
DANIEL K. AKAKA, Hawaii
BYRON L. DORGAN, North Dakota

WILLIAM V. ROTH, JR., Delaware
TED STEVENS, Alaska
WILLIAM S. COHEN, Maine
THAD COCHRAN, Mississippi
JOHN McCAIN, Arizona
ROBERT F. BENNETT, Utah

Leonard Weiss, *Staff Director*
Gordon Hammel, *Investigator*
Franklin G. Polk, *Minority Staff Director and Chief Counsel*
Michal Sue Prosser, *Chief Clerk*

INTERSTATE IDENTIFICATION INDEX: IS IT AN EFFECTIVE WEAPON IN THE WAR AGAINST VIOLENT CRIME? IS IT INTERSTATE, DOES IT IDENTIFY, AND IS IT AN INDEX?

TUESDAY, DECEMBER 6, 1994

U.S. SENATE,
COMMITTEE ON GOVERNMENTAL AFFAIRS,
Washington, DC.

The Committee met, pursuant to notice, at 10:35 a.m., in room SD–342, Dirksen Senate Office Building, Hon. Byron Dorgan presiding.

Present: Senator Dorgan.

OPENING STATEMENT OF SENATOR DORGAN

Senator DORGAN. Ladies and gentlemen, we are going to begin the hearing this morning. My name is Byron Dorgan and I will be chairing the hearing. I appreciate very much the attendance of the people who will provide testimony today, as well as the others who are here.

Let me give a brief introduction as to why I am holding this hearing, why the Committee is interested in this issue, and what I hope to accomplish today. As most of you know, the Senate is not now in session and most Senators are not in Washington, D.C. That doesn't mean that the work of committees does not continue.

I have a deep and abiding interest in one element of law enforcement that was discussed briefly during Congressional debate on the last crime bill. But, in my judgment, we have not provided enough focus and enough direction to this issue, and I have not only worked with the Committee but also with a group called the Advisory Commission on Intergovernmental Relations, a representative of which will testify today, to see what we can do to advance this issue to its logical conclusion.

In 1986, my family was visited by tragedy when my mother was the victim of a manslaughter incident. One person went to prison as a result, but there were several people involved in the incident and I, for the first time in my life, asked for information about the people who were involved. I looked at the public record of the criminal activity of one of the people involved who was not subsequently charged, and I found something that was very startling to me.

This person had been convicted of a crime and had been sent to State prison, released early from State prison, committed another crime—an identical crime, I might add—and was convicted a second time. Although at that point he was on parole and had not finished his first sentence, the judge sentenced him to probation for the second offense. I looked at that and I thought, how on earth could this happen? Someone who should still be in prison is out early, commits a second identical crime, and then is given a sentence of probation. He is not even sent back to prison.

I called the judge who presided in the second case and I said that I was looking at this criminal record and I just wanted to know as a citizen what on earth could have possessed him to decide not to send this person back to prison for the second offense, when he was sent to prison for the first offense. The judge said, after he looked at the background and the papers, "When I sentenced that person, I had no idea that there had been a prior conviction." Whatever information the judge had did not give him the background of this person. So a person who should have been sent to prison was not.

It was my first brush at ever looking at criminal records or understanding how in my State, and I venture to say across the country, that a judge with one phone call would have been able to know whether a person was convicted of a traffic violation—speeding, for example—in any county in my State, but could not, with the same phone call, get information about which felonies had been committed in my State.

I venture to say that, on a national scale if, today, the law enforcement authorities here in the District of Columbia apprehend someone who has been charged and convicted for six separate felony offenses in six separate States, I will wager with most anybody in the room that a check of the central repository of criminal records in this country, the Triple I, will not produce complete records on that criminal.

Why? Because although we are in an age of high technology, the computer age, and although if I buy a shirt this afternoon at a department store they can put my credit card through a magnetic imager and in 20 seconds find out whether my credit card is good, and although they can keep track of a couple hundred million of those credit cards, we have not yet had the public will to decide to keep a computer list of convicted felons in this country that is up to date and complete.

The failure to do so costs lives. The failure to do so is shameful, in my judgment, and we ought not stroll along with some nurturing and some encouragement, hoping that at some point 10, 12, 18 years from now we will have a pretty good computer list of those who commit the crimes in this country. That is not good enough for me.

Most of us know that we have in this country a class of career criminals, in which about 7 percent of the criminals commit about two-thirds of the violent crime. It is unforgivable for us not to know who they are and to keep track of what they have done and where they are. It doesn't take Dick Tracy to figure out who is going to commit the next violent crime. We know who they are. We already have had them in custody, and we ought to keep track of who they are, where they are, and what they have done so that the next judge they come before has full access to all records. This will save lives.

Having said all of that, I have an opening statement I am going to submit for the record that provides evidence of case after case around the country in which someone was apprehended and then allowed to move along because someone didn't have adequate records to even understand who they had apprehended. This person then committed some violent crime that should have been prevented, could have been prevented, would have been prevented had we had a good national computer database of who commits the crimes in this country.

This hearing is not to denigrate the work and the efforts of those who have tried to put this system together. They have developed a partial system which has some good information. We have some dedicated people who very much want this to happen. This is not an attempt to say to those folks, "your work is useless, it has no value." That is not the point at all.

It is to say that it is not enough for me, and I think for the rest of the American people, for us to just stroll along and get there when we will. I want us to get there now. I want this to be an urgent national priority. I want every police officer who apprehends someone to be able to find out quickly who they have apprehended and what they have done in the past. I want every judge who sentences someone to know who they are sentencing and what they have done in every reach of this country. This will save lives.

We have established as part of the National Crime Information Center (NCIC) the assimilation of records into something called the Interstate Identification Index, or Triple I. I know this is a city of acronyms, so forgive me for saying NCIC and Triple I. Triple I means the current computer record database of criminal activity.

Now, where are we heading with this? Well, we are moving to try to get all of the States and all of the jurisdictions within all of the States to send all of their information into one repository where it can be kept on file so that others can access it. It is like every single computer application: if you don't get all the information in, when you access it, you won't get all the information you want out.

We have now, I believe, 21 States who do not provide full, complete records to the Triple I. What does that mean? It means if you are out on the street at midnight and accessing the Triple I, you may not get the information you are looking for. We now only have 20 percent of all of the records complete, including dispositions, that ought to be in the Triple I. What does this mean? It means that you have probably one chance in five of getting all of the records that you wanted if you are accessing the Triple I.

My point is, we need to do much, much better, and we need to do it soon. This needs to be a national urgent priority. This hearing is to demonstrate, first, the need and, second, what we are doing to get to the point where we can, in a matter of a couple of years, say, "We did this. This was a priority. We committed the resources. We did it together." If we get to that point, all of us, I think, can legitimately believe that we have saved lives.

We are putting up a chart of non-participating States, which will show you the states that are not at this point participating in the Triple I. They are still able to access this database of criminal records of by virtue of a cooperative agreement with the FBI. The point is, we don't have everybody at this point moving all of these records of who is committing America's crimes into a database so that it can be used to save lives. The question is: How do we get there, and how do we get there in a hurry?

PREPARED STATEMENT OF SENATOR DORGAN

Today's hearing will focus on the continuing saga of violence committed against society by convicted felons. They are continually released from prison—many of them years early, only to commit more violent and heinous crimes. The worst of these criminals direct their attention to helpless minor children. You can't avoid them—these criminals and their violence have touched every community in this country.

This is not an aberration. This is not about one or two victims who happened to be in the wrong place at the wrong time. This is about a crime epidemic.

There are those that say Americans are so exposed to this type of story—that they are becoming desensitized—that they are ambivalent—that they are no longer outraged by revelations of this nature.

That's just not so! Decent, law-abiding Americans in my State of North Dakota and from every state in this Nation are outraged, as am I. The problem here is that the citizenry is powerless to do anything about it because in part, the law enforcement community is not equipped to deal effectively with the crime epidemic.

We all agree that the first job of government is to protect our citizens, but let me highlight for you a representative example of some of the more egregious examples of rape and molestation cases that have come to my attention . . . in just the last 6 months.

THE OXFORD COMMERCIAL APPEAL—SEPTEMBER 24, 1994

"Cunning Kidnapper With "Need" For Girls is Target of FBI Hunt"

The FBI launched a nationwide search for a man charged with kidnapping an 8-year-old Oxford, Mississippi, girl from her school earlier this month. In 1980, the assailant was convicted of luring 6- and 8-year-old sisters from away from their parents. The girls were bound and blindfolded with their own clothes, then sexually assaulted in a van. In this case, the assailant spent 14 years in prison and was released in February.

THE SALT LAKE TRIBUNE—AUGUST 20, 1994

Man Charged With Kidnappings, Rapes, Child Abductions, Released on Bail

The man suspected of abducting two Salt Lake City girls was released from jail Friday evening, hours after he was charged with four crimes. James K. Holt, 37, is accused of kidnapping a girl August 5 as she walked to school and sexually abusing her. He is also charged with kidnapping another child 3 days later and raping her.

THE BERGEN RECORD—JULY 14, 1994

Ex-Convict Found Guilty of Molesting Girl

A man who served 24 years in prison for killing five in-laws was convicted of 29 counts related to the sexual assault of a girl over a 6 year period. The man was paroled in 1974 after being convicted in 1950 of murdering his estranged wife's parents and three other relatives. His wife and a 9-year-old girl were injured in the attack.

THE ARIZONA REPUBLIC—JULY 12, 1994

A repeat child molester faces life sentence

A repeat sex offender pleaded guilty Monday to attacking three East Valley boys earlier this year and will be sentenced in August to life in prison. Joseph Bruce Maxwell, who spent 14 years in prison after a 1976 conviction for two counts of child molestation, pleaded guilty to sexual conduct with a minor, attempted sexual conduct with a minor and attempted sexual assault.

THE BALTIMORE SUN—JUNE 29, 1994

Life Term to Sexual Offender

A man with a history of more than 30 years of sexual offenses and mental disorders was sentenced to life in prison without parole yesterday for attacking a woman in her home last summer. The man, had been released from prison about 6 weeks before the attack after serving most of a 25-year sentence for kidnapping and raping an 11-year-old Columbia girl in 1974. In 1960, the assailant was convicted of assault with intent to rape and sentenced to a 2 year prison term. In 1962, he was sentenced to 12 years in prison on another charge of assault with intent to rape. That was followed by his conviction in 1974.

Tragically, the stories are endless. As I stated earlier, this is not an aberration. What we are faced with here constitutes a crime epidemic. The common thread with respect to all of these felons is lack of comprehensive criminal histories and related information.

There is no fully operational system in place today that tracks convicted felons. There is no way to know the complete criminal history of an individual who has been stopped by the police and may be wanted. There is no way for a sentencing judge to be totally sure that he knows the complete criminal history of the defendant he is about to sentence.

The miracle of communications is that if you have a credit card, they can find out in 20 seconds in a department store whether your card is good—yet with all of the resources of the United States Government available, we cannot identify and track a felon and possibly prevent him from repeating his or her crimes.

It is not likely that if someone committed six felonies in six different states over an extended period, that anyone would know. In fact, it is very unlikely that the information would be, centralized anywhere in the country, and readily accessible to a judge, or to a law enforcement officer.

Approximately two-thirds of violent crimes in the United States are committed by about 7 percent of the offenders. These are people who were in the criminal justice system and were released for various reasons. Many convicted felons would remain in prison if we had access to their complete criminal histories.

A start was made 10 years ago with the creation of the Interstate Identification Index (III). However, in this central repository, designed to provide instant access to the history of repeat offenders of serious crimes, 80 percent of the crininal records of the states are *not* available or accessible to law enforcement officials on an interstate basis.

Though the III was set up in 1984, as part of the National Crime Information Center (NCIC), assimilation of these records into III seems to be proceeding at a slow pace.

As a result, law enforcement agencies are hampered in determining with any certainty the complete history of any one individual's prior felony convictions.

Consequently, agencies involved in the criminal justice system, more often than not, are vulnerable to making decisions that may well result in real risk to their communities.

As a member of the Advisory Commission on Intergovernmental Relations (ACIR), I have asked the staff to coordinate a review of the current system and to determine what we in the Congress can do to accelerate the pace at which all criminal records will become available to law enforcement officials on an interstate basis.

I cannot emphasize enough the importance of getting this system fully operational as soon as possible—each hour we delay another victim—perhaps a child—will fall prey to an unknown evil that has silently moved into their neighborhood.

But we can do better. I want to work closely with Federal, State and local law enforcement officials to ensure that we protect our citizens.

Senator DORGAN. We have three panels today that we are going to hear from. The first panel is Marc Klaas, with the Marc Klaas Foundation for Children. Many of you know the tragic story of the death of Polly Klaas, and he will discuss the circumstances of that in light of this issue, the identification of people who have committed previous crimes.

We have John Walsh, who many of you know is involved with "America's Most Wanted," a program that has done, I think, an enormous public service and has actually led to the apprehension of some very violent criminals in this country.

We have W.C. Brown from the sheriff's office in Jacksonville, Florida.

Let me thank the three of you for coming and let me start with Mr. Walsh, if I might. Let me just ask you a couple of questions, and then I think you have a videotape that you wanted to show us.

Mr. Walsh, I have watched your program and commend you for it. How many violent criminals do you estimate that your program is responsible for capturing?

TESTIMONY OF JOHN WALSH, "AMERICA'S MOST WANTED"

Mr. WALSH. Well, we have been on for 7 years, Senator, and in those 7 years, as a direct result of tips to our hotline, viewer tips, we have been able to apprehend 335 dangerous fugitives, 10 of the FBI's 10 Most Wanted. We have caught people in 22 countries in 7 years, and I think that is a testimonial to the American public and their support of the show.

But I what I wanted to say before we started was I wanted to commend you and your staff, Gordon Hamel and your very competent staff. I have been walking the halls of Congress for 13 years since my son's murder trying to get things changed and trying to see if there was a way that this country, with the resources we have, could somehow facilitate the exchange of information amongst law enforcement.

I think every American would like to see it or is under the false assumption that the police can access this information immediately. So I would say you are right on target and your priorities are in order, so I commend you for having these hearings today. I hope that this brings into the focus the simple fact that law enforcement is so overwhelmed, and this chart right here shows that 21 States don't even put their information into Triple I. So how can a police officer, when he pulls someone over in the middle of the night—and these days, you may not get a driver's license; you are more likely to get a .357 magnum. I believe that police officer ought to be able to find out if that guy is on the FBI's 10 Most Wanted and if he is a dangerous fugitive.

Senator DORGAN. You have worked with State and local law enforcement authorities all over the country, I assume. Is it your firsthand experience that the index we now have is woefully incomplete, that you do not have any real assurance that if you access that index that you are getting the information you need?

You heard my discussion about someone who commits six felonies in six different States and a judge comes along and says, "Well, let's find out who this person is." Are they likely to get all of the records of those six different States and six felonies?

Mr. WALSH. Absolutely not. I mean, woefully incomplete is putting it mildly. I think it is absolutely a disgrace that we expect law enforcement to do so much these days, but we don't give them the resources. You are absolutely right. This problem is on a State level. I am a great believer that the Federal Government can do certain things, force States to do certain things, but this is truly a country of 50 little countries and until there is an exchange of information on convicted felons and fugitives Nationwide, we are putting law enforcement at a great disadvantage.

I have seen it firsthand on "America's Most Wanted." I have seen so many police agencies trying to do their job, apprehend an individual, and in many States unless that individual has identification or there is a suspicion that they have done something wrong, the police can't hold that individual. Even if they feel something has been done wrong and they hold the individual for several hours, sometimes days—and I will show you cases here today where it has been days—they cannot get the adequate information to charge that individual. They may not know until that individual is gone that that individual is wanted for several killings.

Today, what I wanted to show you was a very graphic example of how the system doesn't work, of three serial killers that have criss-crossed this country in the last 2 months randomly killing American citizens and have been apprehended by law enforcement, and because law enforcement didn't have the tools that we were talking about today, these individuals were let go and they went on to kill again. So I would like you to look at this videotape.

Senator DORGAN. All right. Why don't we proceed to watch the clip? How long does it run?

Mr. WALSH. It is about 8 minutes.

[Videotape shown.]

Mr. WALSH. You know, the saddest thing about this is the lack of information of the police agencies, and you are going to hear from the sheriff's department in Jacksonville. Gary Ray Bowles, the gay serial killer, is also a suspect in 13 other slayings. We got tips that he was in a rooming house. The Jacksonville Beach police went there. They didn't have adequate information, they didn't have an updated picture. He had the fake I.D. and they let him go.

The weekend that he was named on the FBI's top 10 as the top 10 fugitive in the Nation, named all over the country, he was in the Jacksonville sheriff's jail that same weekend on a drunk and disorderly charge and was released, and they believe he killed a man 4 days later.

Those two guys, the natural-born killers—Skillikorn was released from jail after serving only 7 years for a homicide, and Niklasson killed his own father when he was 9 years old—repeat offenders with a rap sheet this long picked up for hitch-hiking, one of them kept, by luck, by a good police officer. The San Diego Police actually took Skillikorn back to the highway and let him go, and thank God that we were able to get that on the news broadcasts, et cetera.

I think this is a graphic example of three serial killers traveling around this country, apprehended three times by police and released three times in a row to go out possibly to kill again.

Senator DORGAN. But not because someone in the police force said, "Gee, we don't care much about this." It is because they were operating without basic information that should have told them that they have apprehended a killer.

Mr. WALSH. Absolutely. You are absolutely right. I mean, if you looked at the police in those segments, the Jacksonville police did a great job in catching Gary Bowles, not knowing twice, the Jacksonville police and the Jacksonville Sheriff's Department when they had him, that he was a serial killer simply from lack of information.

I share the frustration that law enforcement has that when they pull someone over, these guys know, and you saw it graphically there—they don't carry any I.D.; they know they are wanted for everything. They have got a rap sheet a mile long. What do they do when you stop them? "I am John Walsh." You run it through the computer and there are no warrants and you don't have the time to get a fingerprint. Sometimes, it takes a week, 10 days, to get a fingerprint, and you know what the laws are like in this country. Unless you have I.D., unless you have reason to hold this person, the law says you can't hold this person, even though many of those cops say, I know this guy is dirty, I know somebody wants this guy; I have got a suspicion, a gut feeling that something is wrong with this individual.

But if you look at the technology that we have in this country—and I speak out of frustration as the father of a murdered child, as you will hear Marc Klaas speak. I am a Florida native and when I see that space shuttle go up to the tune of $4 to $5 billion every time it goes up and they are raising mice in space, and I look at these cops who are saying let me catch these guys, and these guys are running around the country—just like you said, 80 percent of the violent crimes are committed by 10 to 15 to 20 percent of the repeat offenders. Twenty-one States don't even use the system, say they don't have money. We can put a man on the moon, but we can't catch a serial killer that we know what he looks like, we have his fingerprints, we know his identity, and he can go from coast to coast.

When I first really realized how bad this was—after my son's murder, a serial killer by the name of Atis Tuhl confessed to Adam's murder. He is in jail in Florida, and his partner was Henry Lee Lucas, an infamous serial killer from Texas. Several years ago, they were arrested for several murders and they confessed to a lot of murders that they didn't do.

Atis Tuhl got custody of his partially retarded niece. He was the only relative. He and Henry Lee Lucas repeatedly raped her, killed her, and cut her up and put her body parts in their car. Lucas has an IQ of about 95. Tuhl is partially retarded with an IQ of about 87. Neither one had drivers' licenses. They had her body in the trunk of a stolen car with a stolen license plate on it.

They were stopped three times as they went across the country on their crime spree and released for lack of information, and when they were finally caught Henry Lee Lucas, a guy with a 90 IQ, said, I figured out that I could kill a man or a woman or a child in any part of this country because the minute I crossed a county line, I was a safe—not a State line; the minute I crossed a county line, because law enforcement doesn't exchange information. So what happens when you get a smart serial killer like Ted Bundy? He can go coast to coast and kill 30 or 40 women. The FBI estimates that there are probably 30 serial killers out there at large today, identity unknown. Miami is right now suffering under a serial killer spree of about 17 homicides. They don't have a clue of who it is.

The point I am making today is with the resources this country has and the money that this country has, how can we allow these people to go across country and kill our loved ones? If you saw USA

Today yesterday, it said "Random Killings Hit a High." For the first time in the history of this country, you are more likely to be killed by a stranger than be killed by someone that you know. We set an all-time record in this country last year of 24,600 homicides. These people are roaming the country at large. They know that the law enforcement people in this country don't have the training, don't have the money, don't have the resources. And if crime is the number one issue, I can't understand why exchange of information amongst law enforcement and the apprehension of these individuals isn't the number one priority of this Congress and the number one priority of State legislators.

I hope in my lifetime that I see a police officer, for his own protection and for our protection of our loved ones, be able, through his police car, to access someone he pulls over; that he doesn't get out of that police car and take a .357 magnum bullet, like the poor sheriff in Colorado last week who pulled over a car with two known felons, two killers, with a stolen plate. There was all kinds of information; he couldn't get it. He stepped out of that car while his wife was back listening on the radio to police headquarters. He never got his gun out. They shot him four times.

If he had simply known that those two people were on the run and that there were warrants all over the country for them and they were suspects in all kinds of other crimes—I hope I see that in my lifetime, but what you said this morning hit the nail on the head. The lack of exchange of this information absolutely, without a doubt, costs lives, and you are going to hear from this man that it cost him the life of his daughter.

Senator DORGAN. Mr. Walsh, your interest and concern and dedication to this issue is borne of personal tragedy in your family, and I appreciate very much your willingness to come and testify. The film you showed underscores that this is not theory. This is not some abstraction that we discuss with pipes in our mouths and our feet up. This is an issue that is costing lives.

It is, in my judgment, unforgivable that we sloganeer about crime when we get involved in the politics of creating a crime bill, but we don't do the fundamental things to decide in this country we will keep a computer list of those who have committed the crimes so that we know who they are, where they are, what they have done, so that judges know, police officers know, probation officers know. It is unforgivable that we don't have that information, and the failure to have it is costing lives in this country.

I am determined one way or another to see that we find a way, instead of moseying along to the future where in 8 years or 10 years or 20 years we may have a system in which 80 percent of the records exist, that it becomes an urgent national priority that in the near future this record exists and it is complete, accurate, and begins to save lives.

So I appreciate very much your being with us. I understand you have to leave.

Mr. WALSH. I am going to stay to listen to my friend, Marc Klaas, and then I have to go. Again, I appreciate the opportunity. I give you lots of credit for having the guts to hold these hearings, and you are going to hear from lots of frustrated law enforcement officers today who say, give us the tools, we want to catch these people.

Senator DORGAN. Let me now turn to Marc Klaas. Marc, you also have been visited by an enormous tragedy with the loss of your daughter. From it is born an interest in trying to help see that it doesn't happen to others. Let me hear your testimony which relates to this issue of keeping track of who has committed criminal acts in this country.

TESTIMONY OF MARC KLAAS,[1] MARC KLAAS FOUNDATION FOR CHILDREN

Mr. KLAAS. Thank you so much, Senator. I believe part of the problem here with not having these data bases or not having this database available is perhaps because it is not what one would call a glamorous type of a criminal anti-crime law. It is not a sentencing law. It is much more mundane in nature, and I think perhaps that is partially why a lot of attention has not been paid to it. However, we have done something in California and I would like to talk to you about that.

America really expressed outrage over the kidnap and murder of my daughter, Polly. She touched the psyche of the Nation. She inspired works of art and poetry. The beautiful face and the grace of her movement made grown men cry. Her tragedy also highlighted many of the inequities in our criminal justice system. She was stolen and murdered by a violent felon with an extensive criminal record who had no right being in society. In Polly's name, and in the name of the numerous other victims, America has expressed outrage and demanded that steps be taken to ensure the safety of our citizens.

As our technological capabilities continue to grow, our society must put more resources into the implementation of the advanced data bases that track and monitor the convicted felons upon their return to society. On the evening of October 1, 1993, sheriff's deputies had Polly's kidnapper in their custody within 2 hours of her abduction. If they had known his criminal history, perhaps Polly would still be alive. I quite frankly think that those deputies are lucky that they are still alive.

Because of Polly's tragic circumstance and the hard work of many dedicated citizens, legislators, and law enforcement officials, California now has a state-of-the-art computer system that will provide exactly that kind of protection. It is called the California Violent Crime Information, Investigation, and Technology Act of 1994. It offers local law enforcement, including officers in the patrol cars, the most potent information resource ever developed to assist in the identification, tracking, apprehension, and prosecution of habitual sexual offenders and repeat violent felons.

The violent crime information network part of this act within the Department of Justice enables crime analysts to electronically share their data, analysis, and findings on violent crime cases with law enforcement, again, in the patrol cars. The violent crime information system tracks and monitors violent offenders and their activities. The sexual habitual offender program profiles and tracks

[1] The prepared statement of Mr. Klaas appears on page 59.

the most serious sexual predators and assists local law enforcement in solving open cases.

The CAL-DNA offender file allows local law enforcement to match DNA samples with all known sexual and violent offenders with samples taken from unsolved cases. In fact, there has already been one cold hit in California much more quickly than they thought they would be able to solve a case with a cold DNA sample.

Now, these efforts should be replicated in every State and that information should be instantaneously accessible through the Triple I. As John was stating, and you, sir, it is as valid for a law enforcement official in Wisconsin to have the same information available as his counterpart in California.

Again, the numbers vary, but a small percentage of the repeat violent offenders commit the large percentage of the violent crimes. One-third of these felons who commit these crimes are transients who roam the country at will. Now, when a previously convicted felon crosses State lines, he knows that he can effectively erase his criminal history. Law enforcement and other agencies involved in the criminal justice system cannot determine with certainty the complete history of a suspect without the resources necessary to perform the task. Therefore, they are unable to make decisions that adequately protect the public, such as your relative, sir, and such as my relative.

States are required by Federal law to spend at least 5 percent of their Byrne formula grant money to improve their criminal justice records systems. The Brady bill authorizes $100 million to be distributed over a 6-year period to computerize State criminal records and ultimately implement an instant check system.

It is the fundamental duty of government at all levels to protect the welfare and lives of innocent citizens. By demanding that our public officials invest the funds, the effort, and the time necessary to provide the advanced computer systems, including the Triple I, we can give law enforcement the tools necessary to protect the public and to protect themselves.

It is our priorities, sir, that are far off line. The painful truth is that junkyard computer automation is more sophisticated than most States' violent crime tracking systems. One would be able to go into a junkyard and get a fender for Richard Allen Davis' Pinto faster than one could find out who Richard Allen Davis was, and that is absolutely pitiful.

It is pretty pathetic, in fact, that junkyards have better information systems than State governments responsible for providing for the public safety. As we approach the 21st century, we deserve a law enforcement capability that utilizes the advanced technology available in the waning years of the 20th century. We must demand that the world that our children inherit from us is safer than the one that we inherited from our parents, and we are not providing that right now, sir.

Thank you.

Senator DORGAN. Mr. Klaas, thank you very much. I appreciate very much your being here and sharing the story that many of us know. It underscores that doing things right in this country can save lives and not doing them right can cost lives. I hope that your contribution will, in the longer term, give us the kind of system that will prevent acts of these types from occurring in the future.

Next, let us hear from Mr. Brown, who is with the Jacksonville Sheriff's Department. Mr. Brown, welcome.

TESTIMONY OF W.C. BROWN,[1] DIRECTOR OF OPERATIONS, OFFICE OF THE SHERIFF, JACKSONVILLE, FL

Mr. BROWN. Thank you, Senator. Senator, I think it has already been said by these other two gentlemen that our biggest problem is the lack of information sharing. It is not that local law enforcement or State or Federal law enforcement don't want to share the information. It is just the fact that we don't have the ability to share.

A case in point is the Bowles case that was on the film. This is an excellent example that just occurred a few weeks ago. This was an individual who was wanted by Florida, Georgia, and Maryland for murder. He was on the top 10 of the FBI's Most Wanted list, on national media, and so forth. He was arrested in Duval County, in Jacksonville, on a misdemeanor charge, used an alias. We ran his fingerprints through our local AFIS system, our automated fingerprint identification system, and since he did not have a local record, he was cleared for release and was released from jail. Within 4 days, he had committed another murder.

We were then looking for this individual under his alias, made the arrest, and during the interview he confessed to his true identity and to six other murders. As John testified, he is a suspect in many other murders as well.

Senator DORGAN. Let me interrupt your testimony there. It is not my intention to put you on the spot for this at all because I understand what happened, but when you apprehend someone and check fingerprints, you say you are checking it against a local file. How long would it take you to check it against the fingerprint files of the FBI?

Mr. BROWN. That would take weeks.

Senator DORGAN. So you cannot keep someone——

Mr. BROWN. Not on a misdemeanor charge. In fact, on a misdemeanor charge such as he was charged with, disorderly, those fingerprints would not have even been sent to Washington.

Senator DORGAN. I see.

Mr. BROWN. We would have had no idea who this individual was, and I would submit to you that this is not an isolated occurrence. This is happening elsewhere as well. What many of us in law enforcement would like to see is the sharing of information on the local, State, and national level.

When we start looking at the individuals who use aliases, it compounds the problem even further. The only way to identify these people is through fingerprints, so I would strongly suggest to you as part of the Triple I program that a national automated fingerprint system be looked at as well. The technology is there.

Case in point: we have a $4 million AFIS system in our police building. Six blocks up the road, FDLE has a like AFIS system and they are not networked either. We just do not share information.

[1] The prepared statement of Mr. Brown appears on page 67.

Still, we have the same mentality in many departments, many States around this country that crime stops at the county line. We don't share from county to county, from State or State, or on the national level. Criminals are more mobile now than they have ever been in the past. We have to have a means of tracking and identifying these people.

Senator DORGAN. Have you completed your testimony?

Mr. BROWN. Yes.

Senator DORGAN. Mr. Brown, thank you very much.

Senator DORGAN. Let me ask both you, Mr. Klaas, and Mr. Brown, if—well, let me first ask Mr. Brown, from a law enforcement standpoint, is there a set of criteria by which we ought to be checking identities across the country? Let's assume that we get an adequate database and that database represents all of the relevant criminal files so that you could access them quickly. Do we currently have procedures in place that would mean people who are apprehended would be tracked adequately through that?

I mean, you talk about how often people would provide an alias, so you don't have fingerprint opportunities for several weeks. On a misdemeanor, you wouldn't even proceed with fingerprints to the FBI, is that correct?

Mr. BROWN. Yes, sir. In the future—and from what I understand, the technology exists today of actually rolling a print in a car being sent over the air waves to a central station and then faxed on up to Washington, and you can get a response back within a couple of minutes. That technology exists today. The use of aliases—the only way to combat that is through fingerprints, or possibly DNA some time down the road, but it is a serious problem for us.

Senator DORGAN. Mr. Klaas, the circumstance of your daughter's death was, as you testified, that the person was apprehended a couple of hours after the abduction. At that point, did he provide an alias?

Mr. KLAAS. No, sir. In fact, he gave them his real name. Had there been the technology act that we now have in California in place at that time, they would have been able to identify him in a couple of different ways, through his driver's license, through his vehicle registration, through a physical description and identifying marks.

They did have his real name. They did check into his background and all they were able to determine was that there were no present warrants out for his arrest. Therefore, they let him go. The circumstances were so incredible, though, that if they had realized that they were dealing with a twice-convicted kidnapper with a rap sheet that ran back to age 12, they most certainly would have had reason to bring him in.

It was on a private rural road. It was midnight and he did say that he was sight-seeing at the time. I mean, it is just absolutely mind-boggling that they did let him go. I feel that they are lucky that they are alive, though. They had no idea what they were dealing with. I mean, if nothing else, you know, besides saving citizens' lives, it certainly will offer police the protection that they need so that they will know who they are dealing with oftentimes in these cases.

86-004 O - 95 - 2

Senator DORGAN. But I have seen the arrest record of Mr. Richard Allen Davis and it is very lengthy.

Mr. KLAAS. Yes, sir.

Senator DORGAN. Incarceration, arrest, conviction, release—very, very lengthy. That was not accessible by the officers who apprehended him that evening?

Mr. KLAAS. No, sir, it was not at all. In fact, there was a law that was passed in 1984 which did provide that information, but it lost its funding just a couple of years later. In fact, the technology act that we have right now, the VCIN act, in California is really just an updating of that law that is now going to provide permanent funding for it.

Senator DORGAN. But even if that had been accessible in California, you could conceivably have a person who had committed all of those acts in Nevada, and if you didn't have a national database, you could access the California computer list and not discover what you were looking for.

Mr. KLAAS. That is absolutely correct, yes, sir. In fact, none of this information is going to be any good unless it is really taken care of on—you have to start on the local level and everybody is going to have to be feeding information into this database. Every time somebody gets out of prison, the corrections department is going to have to share it with the Department of Justice so that they can put it into their computers and then send it to the Triple I. No question about that.

Senator DORGAN. Well, I assume—and I would ask Mr. Brown this question—I assume that in law enforcement there is a lot of activity on the front end to try to search for and apprehend criminals. I mean, that is what law enforcement is about.

Mr. BROWN. Yes, sir.

Senator DORGAN. But the requirement day-to-day and week-to-week to maintain a database is sort of part of the dusty duties in the back room of taking the arrests, taking the disposition of the case, keying it into some sort of computer record, making it a part of the files. That costs money. The case is over. The person is arrested. The person is in jail. Now, we are going to spend money to try to take those records and move them someplace. Instead, you spend your money out there on the beat because you are trying to protect people. So the result is—it is true, this person is arrested, convicted, put away, and the record now is in a file someplace.

The person that is put away gets out on parole and an officer stops the person the next week and that record is in a file, but not part of the computer. That officer then checks with the computer, Triple I, and finds out, this person has no record.

Mr. BROWN. Senator, you are absolutely correct, and what we are faced with is most of these cases are made by local law enforcement. There are many counties throughout this country—there are many in the State of Florida in the 67 counties that we have that are not computerized at all. Everything is done manually in small agencies. You are absolutely right. They make the arrest and they put the perpetrator in jail, but the follow-up work and the imputting of all the records is non-existent.

Senator DORGAN. It is a cost?

Mr. BROWN. It is a cost, yes, sir.

Senator DORGAN. Do you think people are dying as a result of this?

Mr. BROWN. Absolutely. I can prove that point to you from a recent case in Jacksonville that was just discussed.

Senator DORGAN. The point that was made on the tape by Mr. Walsh was not, I think I indicated earlier, intended to cast a reflection at all on the sheriff's office because this was a circumstance where I think—and you have described it—you didn't have any idea who you had in custody.

Mr. BROWN. Absolutely not, and the fact remains the same thing could be happening today. There is no safeguard in effect now that would prohibit from happening again what happened last month. There is none.

Senator DORGAN. You know, it is interesting that the only real meaningful debate we have had on this subject has really not been conducted in the context of law enforcement. The only debate on a national records check system has had to do with the Brady bill, saying that a gun store owner out there selling a handgun ought to be able to access—just as a department store does with a credit card, ought to be able to access some database to find out whether a person is a felon and therefore should not be sold a gun. That is the only real meaningful debate we have had about a national computer record of felons, which to me is unfathomable.

This is the centerpiece, it seems to me, of allowing law enforcement to work. I have not talked today about tracking pedophiles, for example. Somebody moves into your neighborhood and has six priors with child sexual abuse. Should we know they moved into the neighborhood? You are darned right we should.

Mr. KLAAS. First of all, he shouldn't even be on the street.

Senator DORGAN. He shouldn't be on the street. I don't disagree with that, but my point is we just don't have the capability right at the starting gate to adequately provide the law enforcement functions that we should with respect to those that commit repeat violent acts in our society.

Mr. BROWN. Senator, I think we have the capability. I believe what we are lacking is other members other than yourself with vision that will push the point. The capability is there, the technology is there. The leadership of people like yourself taking a leadership role in combatting the crime problem is what we are lacking, and I congratulate you for——

Senator DORGAN. With respect, I don't even think it is that. There is $100 million that now exists for precisely this function, and I am told that we previously had $26 million or so, and some of it wasn't even spent because it is a matter of will and a matter of urgency not just on the part of someone here, but on the part of someone in some county some place or some city some place that says it is important for us in our city, county, or State to decide to be a full participating partner in this computer base of felons.

It costs money, but we now have $100 million available and my guess is, even if we spend that, 6 years from now we will not have an adequate and accurate database. So, what I am trying to get at today is: how do we not only not wait 6 years, but also how do we at the end of a much shorter period have a database that contains the felons in this country for purposes of law enforcement and judges.

Mr. KLAAS. Certainly, the people in this country should demand that their officials do the job that they were elected to do. It is really a matter of misplaced priorities, like we have mentioned time and again. Legislators get paid well. Legislators drive around in nice cars. They have full health benefits and they have great pensions. That is terrific for them, but they were not put in there to surround themselves with the trappings of power. They were put into positions of power—and, in fact, I think this is maybe part of the reason that things changed so much a couple of weeks ago, because people are fed up with the fact that we keep electing the same people time and time again.

They go in and there are a lot of great words. Everybody talks a good game, but nobody is doing a whole lot about it, and we are just throwing away the future of this country. People are getting killed randomly. As John just stated, for the first time in our history we have more random killings than, I guess, pre-meditated. It is absolutely unbelievable.

We seem to be making steps toward putting these people away and keeping them in jail, and we are starting to get truth in sentencing in some places, but once they are out on the street, I mean it is carte blanche for these characters and they commit these crimes time and time and time again. What is so pitiful is, as you stated, sir, we know exactly who they are. We know exactly who they are.

Senator DORGAN. But, Mr. Klaas, the dilemma here is some interpret the elections, and I think probably not inaccurately so, as saying that people want less government, less Federal Government involvement, especially. I just showed you the chart that shows that some 21 States have on their own volition decided that we are not going to participate in the Triple I.

Well, the only way one would conceivably get those States to do it is either on a voluntary basis by saying "You have to do this. We really need those records—if somebody is committing murders in one of those states that doesn't contribute, the rest of it won't know it and so it hurts the rest of us." Or you mandate the States to do it by saying, "We mandate you to do it. Here is some money, but we require you to do it." Well, that is the heavy hand of the Federal Government once again, and that is the dilemma we have.

But the fact that we have not yet completed this project and we are not even well down the road—I guess the fact is that a lot of people don't want us to do anything more than urge someone else to do this. Let's urge them, let's coax them, let's encourage them, let's not require them. That is why you have 21 states that are not now participating in the Triple I. That is the question we have to address.

Mr. KLAAS. And there are 21 governors and 21 attorneys general that are going to have take it upon themselves to do this, sir.

Senator DORGAN. That is correct, but what if they don't?

Mr. KLAAS. If they don't, then kick them out. I mean, I don't think that there are too many people that are going to argue the fact that information that was initially public to begin with on these people—I mean, everybody that has been sent to jail has had it in the newspaper that they have committed these crimes and been put in jail. What is the problem with collating this information, putting it in a database used to protect innocent citizens? I mean, I don't think anybody is going to argue that.

Senator DORGAN. I share your impatience. We are long past the time where we ought to establish this as a national, urgent priority. If this isn't a priority, we don't need any more crime bill debates because this must be a priority in order for us to give the law enforcement people the tools to apprehend violent criminals.

Mr. KLAAS. We have nothing to be proud of as a country until we can do that. We can sit there, like John said, and salute the space shuttle all day long, but as long as we allow these creeps, these monsters, to roam the streets and commit these crimes with impunity, then we have nothing to be proud of. We should be ashamed.

Senator DORGAN. Mr. Brown, do you have anything to add?

Mr. BROWN. No. Thank you, Senator.

Senator DORGAN. Mr. Brown, I appreciate your coming up from Florida and Mr. Klaas coming over from California today to give testimony.

Mr. KLAAS. Thank you, sir.

Senator DORGAN. We would like to keep in touch with you. Thank you very much.

I would like to call the next panel. Max Krupo, the Assistant Chief of Police in the D.C. Police Department; Mr. William Davis from the Advisory Commission on Intergovernmental Relations; and Major James V. Martin with an organization called SEARCH.

As you are coming forward, I would like to thank Seth Benjamin with the ACIR for the efforts that he has made, and let me thank the three of you for coming today. Let me begin with you, Mr. Krupo. Fred Thomas, the D.C. Police Chief, was going to be with us today and he apparently is in some budget meetings today. We are well aware that those meetings are going on by reading the local newspaper.

Mr. Krupo, I thank you for being present in his stead and why don't you proceed?

TESTIMONY OF MAX J. KRUPO,[1] ASSISTANT CHIEF OF POLICE, METROPOLITAN POLICE DEPARTMENT, WASHINGTON, DC

Mr. KRUPO. Good morning. I am Assistant Chief of Police Max Krupo, the technical services officer of the Metropolitan Police Department for the District of Columbia. I am very pleased to have this opportunity to represent Chief of Police Fred Thomas on this very important issue surrounding our efforts to identify the new breed of mobile criminal who is preying on our communities throughout this Nation. Chief Thomas regrets he was unavailable to attend this hearing.

Let me say at the outset that the Metropolitan Police Department fully supports the Triple I program. We have been working toward the full implementation of all aspects of Triple I. An unrelated ordinance and court ruling in the early stages of this project severely restricted the District of Columbia's participation. How-

[1] The prepared statement of Mr. Krupo appears on page 51.

ever, in 1989, with the help of the City Council and Congress, we were able to establish legislation that opened the way for full participation. Since that time, efforts have been underway to create a fully automated criminal records system within our jurisdiction.

This task has not been easy, since it requires the complete cooperation of all the criminal justice agencies within the District of Columbia to record and report their criminal records information at one central database. However, heretofore, each agency was able to maintain their own individual record systems. The systems were manual and in many cases contained outdated information.

The Triple I program has no room for inaccurate recordkeeping which could result in the loss of a person's constitutional rights. We in law enforcement are well aware of the sensitivity of data on repeat violent offenders and the implications for our failure to safeguard that data. Our standards for recordkeeping are far more stringent than for any other profession. We cannot tolerate the plus or minus 10 percent error rate which is acceptable in other industries or professions. Our systems must provide instantaneous information that is unquestionably accurate, while at the same time providing complete and positive identification of the subject of record. Few, if any, other systems on this earth require that level of accuracy.

We in law enforcement accept and understand the need for such a mandate. However, in an era characterized by shrinking budgets and increasing demands for services, we are in a systems development battle. You may be assured that the completion of the Triple I program is at the top of our list.

Development on the Triple I program has been progressing and will continue to be developed with the greatest of effort. We expect that the Metropolitan Police Department will have established full membership of the Triple I program by December of 1995.

On June 20th of 1994, Attorney General Janet Reno directed a memorandum to the mayor of the District of Columbia wherein she established minimum mandatory dates for compliance with the National Child Protection Act of 1993 and the Brady Handgun Violence Prevention Act. The dates established by the Attorney General were arrived at after a consultation with the Metropolitan Police Department and are consistent with how fast we feel that an orderly transformation of our criminal records system can be accomplished. This type of cooperation between the Federal Government and the respective State agencies has been the norm for this process, and I can State that this spirit is what has made our other law enforcement information systems so successful.

However, it must stated that in the eyes of police officers there is a huge difference between a criminal arrest record and a criminal history record. While our goal is to create an automated system where each record is complete, with all available information from the courts, paroles and corrections systems, I feel that we cannot reach that stage for some time.

However, we can and will reach an interim goal where at least criminal arrest information will be available for immediate law enforcement uses. The value of preliminary arrest data cannot be overstated. Many times, preliminary arrest information on a subject can make a difference as to the level of scrutiny that individual receives during the course of an investigation. Certainly, the individual's rights must be protected and final dispositions are needed for longer-term investigations and court sentencing, but the mere fact that an individual was arrested is generally in most jurisdictions already a matter of public information.

We in the Metropolitan Police Department are moving to complete a system whereby the much needed preliminary arrest information I have been speaking about can be provided to law enforcement personnel, as required under the guidelines of Triple I. We are in concert, and have received full support from the FBI on this project. Without their assistance, we would not be as advanced as we are.

As one of the original members of the SEARCH group who helped conceive this idea of a Triple I, I can State that we envisioned the Cadillac of systems. We were advised by the technocrats at that time that every feature and capability we wanted was within our reach. However, I sit before you today, 10 years later, certain in the knowledge that there are many problems when you try to standardize multiple automated systems.

In hindsight, I think it is fair to say that we underestimated the massive technical requirements needed to take this process from concept to reality. As time goes on and we continue development with current and future technology, these standardization problems will become a thing of the past. Given the direction of automated fingerprint systems in this Nation, I feel confident that the days where a criminal could sneak through the system merely by changing his name and growing a beard have come to a close. In the future, we will see imaging systems that allow law enforcement officers to positively identify suspects on the street from their patrol cars, in partnership with technology.

In closing, let me State for the record that while the development of this system has been agonizingly slow, we have not been sitting on our hands. Since 1989, the Metropolitan Police Department alone has submitted approximately 80,000 criminal arrest records, supported by fingerprints, to the FBI for inclusion into the Triple I system. The FBI has diligently worked with the MPD in this process and I am confident that our most serious criminals can, as a result, be located by other law enforcement agencies throughout the United States.

The MPD is currently classified as a participant in Triple I, which means we can make inquiries into the system and receive responses. However, our records are not yet automated enough to allow us to be classified as full members and exchange information with other agencies through the automation of the Triple I system.

This problem is being addressed as we speak. Programmers are more than 70 percent complete in their efforts to complete the necessary interfaces. Data entry personnel are working tirelessly to convert 700,000-plus existing manual records into a computer-readable format and the booking officers are being trained. I fully expect that the MPD will meet the guidelines set forth in the previous specified legislation and those further defined by the Attorney General.

Thank you for the opportunity to appear before this body. I hope that my testimony has helped ease the concerns that any members may have had concerning the design and implementation of the most comprehensive information system ever developed for law enforcement. I would be happy to answer any questions that the panel may have at this time.

Senator DORGAN. Mr. Krupo, thank you very much. If you would be willing to stay with us, I would like next to hear from Mr. Martin and then Mr. Davis, after which I will ask some questions.

Mr. Martin, you are with the Statistical Electronic Analysis of Criminal Records Histories, which has an acronym of SEARCH. Would you, when you begin, tell us how SEARCH is funded and organized?

TESTIMONY OF JAMES V. MARTIN,[1] ASSISTANT DIRECTOR, SOUTH CAROLINA LAW ENFORCEMENT DIVISION, ON BEHALF OF THE NATIONAL CONSORTIUM FOR JUSTICE INFORMATION AND STATISTICS

Mr. MARTIN. All right, sir. First, SEARCH is the National Consortium for Criminal Justice Information and Statistics. It is funded primarily through the payment of State dues. We have all 50 States, the Virgin Islands, Puerto Rico, and the District of Columbia as members of SEARCH. We have a board of directors which I do serve on. We meet twice a year to discuss various needed policies and issues dealing with criminal justice information.

But I do come here also representing my agency, the South Carolina Law Enforcement Division, too, Mr. Chairman, but I am pleased to be here on behalf of SEARCH to testify on an issue that I feel of vital importance to the war against crime, and that is the cost-effective and efficient interstate exchange of criminal history information for criminal justice and authorized non-criminal justice purposes.

SEARCH has submitted written testimony for the record and, with your permission, I would like to take just a few moments to highlight that testimony. As I said earlier, SEARCH is a non-profit criminal justice organization chartered by State criminal justice officials and it is supported in part by State dues and governed by an assembly of governor appointees from each of the 50 States, the District of Columbia, Puerto Rico, and the Virgin Islands.

For over a quarter of a century, SEARCH has been a voice for the States on law and policy and for criminal justice information. SEARCH's voice has been especially strong in supporting the creation and speedy and complete implementation of the Interstate Identification Index, or Triple I. Accordingly, SEARCH is delighted to testify, and we applaud your interest and leadership and your staff's outstanding efforts to date.

I want to also recognize and credit the extraordinary work of the FBI in adopting the Triple I and working actively and effectively for its full implementation. I would also take this opportunity to applaud the indispensable contribution to the Triple I made by the FBI's Advisory Policy Board, APB, and you will be hearing from that chairman, P.J. Doyle, later this morning.

I serve not only as the governor's appointee to SEARCH and chairman of our Law and Policy Committee, but also as a member

[1] The prepared statement of Mr. Martin appears on page 72.

of that APB, and thus I am doubly proud of the work of both SEARCH and the APB in acting as catalysts and leaders for the development of the Triple I.

I have been with the South Carolina Law Enforcement Division for 18 years, of which 13 has been directly responsible for the operation of the State's criminal records repository, as well as the statewide law enforcement communications system. The national criminal history system is not without flaws and it is far from perfect, but I must emphasize to you how improved the system is today over what it was when I began my career with the Division in 1976.

If you will bear with me, Mr. Chairman, I would like to deviate a little bit from my prepared remarks and comment on some of the things that I have heard from the previous panel. I would like to say that I feel it is important to make the distinction between what was shown in the video and talked about. I feel like that deals with the current national programs or hot files that we talk about. We talk about stolen vehicles, missing persons, and wanted persons.

There is an initiative undertaken right now that is well into the implementation stage, NCIC 2000. In law enforcement, we have had a problem with positive identification and that is some of the problem that we saw in the video. It has very little to do with Triple I, per se, but we have long in law enforcement recognized a problem when encountering a hitchhiker on the interstate with little identification or any at all, wanting to know who that individual was.

Under NCIC 2000, there will be the capability to put fingerprints along with that wanted person's record and have mobile digital devices in those patrol cars so that that individual can be required to input his fingerprints or her fingerprints. It will do a fingerprint match against that national file so we can hopefully make an I.D. on that person. We won't have to rely on aliases and all this false identification that we are being given day in and day out.

The other initiative that I think needs to be talked about as far as positive identification when someone is arrested and we want to know who he or she really is is the integrated automated fingerprint identification initiative that is also underway with the FBI. I would encourage funding for this very important project. What it is is actually, as you may know, moving the identification division from the Bureau here in Washington to Clarksburg, West Virginia. That is well underway.

I am sure the FBI will be able to brief you more in detail on that at your convenience, but basically it is going to allow us to take fingerprints from someone incarcerated, and on an emergency basis we will be able to get a response within 2 hours and know who that individual is. Routinely, they will be able to process criminal justice fingerprints for normal arrests within 24 hours, and it goes on as far as benefits that can be derived from the integrated automated fingerprint identification system project that is underway now. There is no end to the capabilities of that system.

Now, returning to my prepared testimony, we have evolved from a single entity, the FBI's Identification Bureau providing criminal history record information by simply typing rap sheets and mailing them back to the State repositories. Then we moved to a limited automated information system called Computerized Criminal History back in the mid–1970's, and now we are at the stage of Triple I.

Currently, 29 States, I believe, participate in the Triple I system and they actually are direct record providers, which means that they are responding to criminal justice requests for their Triple I index records for local, State, and Federal criminal justice agencies Nationwide. Numerous other State repositories plan to begin participating as record providers within the next few years, and all States have plans for their repository to join Triple I at some future time.

I think it is important for us to recognize a State may not participate as a record provider in Triple I, but all States do have online access to the records indexed in Triple I, so in some cases it is a one-way street. We, of course, prefer for it to be a two-way street in sharing that information.

At present, Triple I provides access to over 21 million criminal records. Of these, approximately 12 million are maintained by participating State repositories and the balance of 9 million are maintained by the FBI. Over 1,756,000 inquiry transactions are processed each month. On the average, one out of every three inquires results in a positive response, and these responses even under the current system are routinely handled within five seconds.

Through Triple I and the FBI's National Crime Information Center's Nationwide communication network and the National Law Enforcement Telecommunications System, approximately 500,000 criminal history records are provided to criminal justice agencies each month throughout the Nation.

When Triple I is completed and fully operational, it can and will provide the criminal justice system with a reliable and near instantaneous means of obtaining a complete and accurate criminal history profile of Federal, State, and local offenders. It will also provide authorized non-criminal justice requestors with an effective and reliable system to access national criminal history information.

It can also reduce costs arising from reporting multiple and subsequent arrests and dispositions to the FBI. It can reduce FBI costs arising from the maintenance of duplicative and redundant State criminal history record information which is being done today. It can also improve the accuracy and completeness of criminal history record information by keeping the records at the State level and making State repositories entirely responsible for the accuracy and completeness of their particular records.

While much progress has been made in implementing Triple I and achieving these benefits, a great deal more needs to be done. There remain many challenges. Twenty-one jurisdictions still do not participate in Triple I and some of the states that are participating do so only at a rather minimal level; that is, they have not assumed responsibility for all of the offenders from their States whose records are maintained by the FBI. In order to participate, many of these States need to further automate their criminal records systems and meet those Triple I standards.

Another major concern that must be addressed is the completeness of the criminal records provided through Triple I. There are a number of factors that affect the completeness of the criminal history record information, in my opinion. My experience leads me to the belief that a primary factor in criminal history record information containing only arrest information is that other components of the criminal justice system have not progressed with automation at the rate law enforcement has.

Most State criminal history record systems were developed by law enforcement; they are managed and maintained by law enforcement. The prosecution, the courts, corrections, probation, and other components of the criminal justice system generally have not had the resources of criminal justice to assist in submitting much-needed case disposition information to the State repositories.

I believe we are experiencing a change in this area. I am of the opinion significant improvements in the timeliness and completeness of criminal history record information in the future will be realized. This will not be easy and it will not be free. Funding will be required. How much funding and for what period of time is truly a difficult question. This is dependent on the status of a particular State system.

Funding made available through the $27 million National Criminal History Improvement Program was used to automate various levels of courts in my State. This significantly improved criminal history in South Carolina. Additional funding is needed to further this effort. I believe such automation can result in similar benefits in many other States.

Other initiatives that will assist in improving the criminal history record system will be expanding the use of automation and the integration of existing automation within the States to create a unified criminal justice system encompassing law enforcement, prosecution, courts, corrections, and probation agencies.

There is a need to establish more training programs for all components of the criminal justice system, not just law enforcement. It is recognized we need to improve our criminal history system, but sadly we often find that the information available today through over 100,000 criminal justice computer terminals throughout this country is simply not being utilized, and we have heard about that this morning. No inquiry is being made.

While it is not necessary for each and every officer on the street to understand how Triple I operates and how the NCIC hot files operate, it is important to understand the limitations of the data and to know how, when, and where to go to seek additional information.

Perhaps the most critical challenge before Triple I is to develop this system for non-criminal justice purposes. Currently, Triple I is used exclusively for criminal justice purposes, with the only exceptions being in the area of national security and certain firearms licensing. The Triple I system has an enormous amount of work to do before the system is available for expanded authorized non-criminal justice use. Until such time as the system is available for authorized non-criminal justice use, the FBI must continue to maintain a comprehensive, redundant criminal history record system.

Before the Triple I can be fully implemented and decentralized, Triple I must provide authorized non-criminal justice requestors with the same level of criminal history record service that they now obtain from the FBI through the submission of fingerprint cards. Backgrounds which include a criminal records check for school teachers, day care center workers, foster parents, and a number of other professions are becoming the norm. The National Child Protection Act has the potential of generating significant numbers of criminal history background checks for non-criminal justice purposes.

The demand for criminal history information in conjunction with non-criminal justice employment is expected to increase with each passing year. Triple I, in my opinion, can assist tremendously in sharing criminal history information between States for such purposes. This will be shared only on fingerprint-supported multi-State offenders.

It is important to recognize that we are not advocating that Triple I become what is often referred to as a Big Brother computer, where someone simply enters a name, date of birth, race, sex, gets either a complete criminal history or an incomplete criminal history and makes some employment decision. Triple I would only be used for non-criminal justice purposes where a record has been established by the FBI through the creation of a uniform FBI number, and only then would that information be allowed to be shared through the Triple I system for making those kinds of employment decisions.

This brings up the next subject that I would like to discuss, the Triple I compact. In addition to amending State laws, a governing charter for the non-criminal justice use of Triple I must be developed, to include a policymaking mechanism. Although this could be accomplished through Federal legislation or uniform State law, a strong consensus has emerged that the best way to accomplish this is to adopt an interstate Federal-State compact.

The advantages of a compact are that it must be ratified in identical form by all parties and, after ratification, cannot be unilaterally amended. Ratifying parties can withdraw only through some formal action and compacts take precedence over conflicting State or Federal law. The Triple I compact has been endorsed by the APB and SEARCH, as well as approved by the FBI Director and the U.S. Attorney General.

As we understand it, the compact is currently at OMB. It is certainly our hope that it will reach the Congress early in 1995. Mr. Chairman, we urge your leadership and support for the compact so that it can be enacted by the Congress in order to authorize FBI participation. We would then hope that the State legislatures could begin adopting the compact perhaps as early as 1995.

Once the compact has been adopted, States will still have discretion as to how much criminal history record information is released to in-State non-criminal justice requestors. On the other hand, those non-criminal justice requestors who have been receiving the full record from the FBI will continue to be able to obtain this level of service through the Triple I system.

Under the Brady Act, the Attorney General has designated the Triple I as the platform for the National Instant Check System which, as you know, must be in place no later than November 1998. This is a welcome development in that it puts further pressure on the States to upgrade their criminal history record systems and to participate in Triple I. Just as importantly, this provides Federal financial resources for this enhancement and Triple I participation.

We have come a long way. We still have a long way to go and, relatively speaking, a very short period of time in which to get there. This hearing, Mr. Chairman, comes at a critical time. One of the famous quips associated with Yogi Berra is that when you get to the fork in the road, take it. In my opinion, we are at the fork in the road and we can either take the fork now that will lead to rapid, effective, and comprehensive implementation of Triple I or we can take the fork that regresses and let the opportunity for the establishment of an effective, decentralized, reliable national criminal history record system slip away.

Thank you again, Mr. Chairman, for your interest and leadership, and I too will field questions following the next speaker.

Senator DORGAN. Mr. Martin, thank you very much.

Next, let us hear from Mr. William Davis the Executive Director of the Advisory Commission on Intergovernmental Relations.

Mr. Davis?

TESTIMONY OF WILLIAM E. DAVIS, III,[1] EXECUTIVE DIRECTOR, UNITED STATES ADVISORY COMMISSION ON INTERGOVERNMENTAL RELATIONS

Mr. DAVIS. Thank you, Mr. Chairman. As you have said, I am Executive Director of the United States Advisory Commission on Intergovernmental Relations. I want to thank you for the opportunity to appear here and speak for the Commission, and particularly its Chairman, William Winter.

The Commission, as you know, was established as an independent bipartisan agency. It is focusing on monitoring and recommending improvements to the American Federal system. The 26 members of the Commission are members of the House, the Senate, appointees of the President from his administration, governors, mayors, State legislators, county officials, and citizen members.

Our attention to criminal justice as a topic began in the 1970's when we did a series of studies on the Safe Streets Act. During the 1980's, we conducted a number of studies on local jail issues, and indeed most recently we have published a two-volume guide to the criminal justice system that is specifically directed for the use of elected officials in Federal, State, and local government.

Our current attention is focused in this criminal justice area on the Interstate Identification Index. As a result of some early examination of this topic, the Commission adopted a work agenda which was intended to help stimulate the full implementation of Triple I. Since that point, we have met with the Department of Justice, the FBI, and a number of other organizations, including the National Governors Association, to determine what steps an intergovernmental organization like the Commission might make in order to assist the development of a comprehensive, complete, and accurate felon registry database.

The challenge before us clearly is in the numbers. As we have heard before, there are only 29 States currently participating in the

[1] The prepared statement of Mr. Davis appears on page 52.

system, and even with this number of States, of the 50 million criminal justice records Nationwide, Triple I contains about 18 million, 9 million of which are complete records, including having an indication of court disposition.

This occurs, as has been said, despite the fact that we have provided substantial Federal assistance to create this system. $27 million was made available in the Anti-Drug Abuse Act of 1988. It does appear to us that a good bit of that money has not indeed been spent. Although it has been allocated, it hasn't been spent. There was $100 million recently appropriated by the Brady bill, and that indeed has given those who think that it is money that makes the difference here renewed confidence that the progress on this will be substantial.

While the number of States in the system has continued to grow, I think what we are all saying is that the pace of implementation is slow. In looking at this whole subject area, one of the things that was most striking to us is that in search for background information, data analysis, and research on the topic, we have become unaware of any really substantial systematic, objective research that goes to the question of why participants themselves, those who contribute the records, are unable to do so.

It is speculated and it is the view of many that it is a technological issue. In the view of others, it has to do with sort of the agenda at the political level, at the State level. In the case of others, they argue that it goes to the question of benefits. How does this whole system benefit me in terms of my individual jurisdiction or my individual job in my jurisdiction? In other cases, it is argued that it has to do with technical assistance, education, et cetera. My own observation is that there is very little systematic data that tells us what is in the way of this system.

We concluded in our examination of this that we had to focus our effort in three areas. The first is that which I have just spoken about, and that is determining the barriers or impediments to the implementation of Triple I. The second has to do with raising the visibility of the issue, and the third has to do with undertaking specific actions that will stimulate and encourage its implementation.

We have developed a work plan that would call for us to undertake a whole series of activities designed to achieve these goals and we have shared that with you prior to this hearing. As you are aware, one of the things that we have proposed is actually to do a survey of State and local officials, a national survey, to look at barriers and impediments.

The second thing we have proposed doing is holding—the Commission is empowered by its authorizing law to hold hearings, and one of the things we have proposed is to hold a series of national hearings basically to raise the awareness among State and local officials and the public at large on the benefits of Triple I.

We have also planned to undertake a series of cooperative efforts with what we view as relevant State and local government organizations across the country, and I refer here to the National Governors Association, the National Conference of State Legislatures, county and sheriffs associations, the IACP, the Center for State Courts, and a number of other organizations with whom we would hope to collaborate in these activities. They often have provided, through their own enterprises, their own activities, their own conventions, their conferences, their publications, an outlet for enhanced information and more substantial information on this. It is our hope to see that that is accomplished. Finally, we have our own communications media within the Commission that we would expect to use.

We have developed, as I said, a detailed work plan to pursue this effort. Let me assure you, Mr. Chairman, that the Commission views this as extremely important and is committed to provide assistance in this effort in whatever ways that we can to the extent that our resources allow.

One final point, Mr. Chairman. The Triple I, as we have all said, is a voluntary system. No State or local jurisdiction and no individual at a State or local level is obligated by law to contribute criminal records to this system. Thus, the success of this effort, it seems to me, hinges entirely on the effectiveness of intergovernmental cooperation; thus, the interest of the Advisory Commission in this effort. I fear that without a greater degree of that cooperation, it will be a long time before we see a complete, accurate record of criminal histories available to all of us at the State and local level.

Thank you, Mr. Chairman.

Senator DORGAN. Mr. Davis, thank you very much.

Mr. Martin, you are from South Carolina.

Mr. MARTIN. Yes, sir.

Senator DORGAN. I assume in South Carolina, like my State of North Dakota, that you have a requirement that if someone is apprehended for traveling 100 miles an hour in a 55-mile-an-hour speed zone somewhere by a city government law enforcement official, the record of the apprehension and the disposition of it is sent to your State Department of Transportation and becomes part of the record of that driver. Is that correct?

Mr. MARTIN. That is correct.

Senator DORGAN. And that would be true in most States. You would have a reasonable expectation that in almost every State in the country, the drivers' license bureau retains and has, on an updated basis, complete driving records. I happen to know from firsthand experience, years and years ago, of course, that if you are picked up in one part of the State, very soon thereafter your record will change in the State office because somebody is going to send them some information that you were going 65 in a 55.

That seems pretty straightforward, pretty easy to do. It is a mandate that has been required for a long time in most States, but we don't have the same mandate with respect to, in some cases, intrastate, and, certainly, interstate cases to keep track of someone who has committed murders, multiple murders, multiple armed robberies, and so on.

Now, your testimony was very useful testimony, and you are involved in an organization that thinks that Triple I is very useful. Most of us think it is useful. I would ask you this based on your knowledge of where we are and where we are headed. Eventually, we want to get to the point where I can say for the Triple I and essentially all criminal offenses, all felonies, and dispositions of those felonies, just exactly what I said about most States' drivers' license systems. I would like to be able to say that we have a computer system and that all records are in it.

When do you think we will get to the point where all States are participating and where all States are participating sufficiently so that we have some comfort that the criminal records history will be in that computer? Will it be 5 years from now, 2 years from now, 10 years from now, ever?

Mr. MARTIN. I need a crystal ball to answer that.

Senator DORGAN. Give me your best judgment.

Mr. MARTIN. I would think that by the year 2000 we should have all States participating in the Triple I if the appropriate funding is made available. Working through the regional working groups of the FBI, it is my understanding that all non-participating Triple I States have committed to become a Triple I participant.

As I recall, also, those State representatives, those people who work in the trenches like I do, have said if our States don't step forward and become participants, then we would not argue with you if you completely cut our State off from accessing Triple I records. I think that was a unanimous vote. So those States and my counterparts firmly recognize and clearly recognize the importance of participating in Triple I. It is simply that they cannot get the resources at the State level to put together a comprehensive State repository.

You know, it is one thing to receive Federal funding to plant the seed and put the core group there, but that is an ongoing situation that you must fund from now until eternity, and I think that is where the problem is, is most States not wanting to make that step.

Senator DORGAN. Mr. Krupo, I put together a meeting in my office 1 day and I asked all the people who were instrumental in this system at the Federal level—the FBI, Department of Justice folks, a pretty good number of them sitting around in a circle in my office—and had a long discussion about what do we have, where are we headed, and when will we get there. I have to confess that at the end of the meeting, I was fairly dispirited.

There was kind of a disconnection between me and them because they were very proud of what they have done, and I understand why they would be proud of it. As Mr. Martin indicated, you start with zero and you start to try to build. They have now constructed something that is partially constructed and they are saying, "We have come a long way."

My response was, "When are we going to get to where we are supposed to? I really can't see the end line based on this discussion because what you have is a system that, by its definition, requires voluntary participation to be successful—voluntary participation in all of the jurisdictions in the 50 States, if it is to be successful. I can't see from this discussion that we are going to get there any time soon. I can't see, frankly, that this is a national urgent priority. I also can sense that people are going to die in the interim."

You indicated you were involved in the early stages of, I believe, SEARCH and the Triple I, and so on. Tell me, Mr. Krupo, when do you think we are going to get there?

Mr. KRUPO. Well, I have got to agree that absent a crystal ball and adequate resources—but I think individual States will come on, as the others have, at different times. Not only do you have 50 different States; you have 4 or 5 jurisdictions or agencies within each State—the courts, corrections, parole, probation—that must also come on board.

Senator DORGAN. That is correct.

Mr. KRUPO. I think as you look at even states that are participating, you will find the law enforcement guys are the first ones to come on board. They are the guys with the big stick; they get the most attention. They need the data the most; our officers need it.

How quickly? I think it is individual. For instance, I know ours—a lot of them better be on board by 1998. I can tell you that because when the Brady bill kicks in, there are requirements there that are Triple I mirror images, and the only way we are going to enforce the Brady bill is meet all those requirements. So a lot of people better do a lot of work fast.

Senator DORGAN. But as long as it is voluntary, and it is, the question is: Will we ever get there? Now, if someone commits a murder in California, is it anybody's business in Arizona? Of course it is. It was a California crime, the victim was in California, the crime was committed in California, the perpetrator was in California, but does someone in Arizona have an interest in that crime? You better believe it.

Let me give you an example. We had a woman, bless her soul, who used to come out here every year to bring tours of people, bus tours, and she would come to the Capitol steps. Her name was Donna Martz. She would come to the Capitol steps and bring these folks and we would take pictures—North Dakota bus tours—a wonderful woman.

On a quiet Sunday morning in Bismarck, North Dakota, she was coming out of a hotel preparing to drive to her home up in Rock Lake, North Dakota, some several hours' drive, and she was abducted in the parking lot of a hotel in Bismarck, North Dakota, on this quiet Sunday morning and murdered several days later after a horror story. She was murdered by people from Pennsylvania who had walked away from a furlough and murdered a person there, been on a crime spree across the country and abducted someone in North Dakota.

Does someone in North Dakota, with a relatively low crime rate, have an interest in the disposition of a case in Pennsylvania? Absolutely. If someone commits a murder in Pennsylvania, does that affect us? You better believe it does. The epidemic of violent crime in this country doesn't respect geographical borders. It has become a national problem, and it seems to me we need to think through this question.

Mr. Martin, is a mandate inappropriate in these circumstances?

Mr. MARTIN. Probably not.

Senator DORGAN. Or will we get there with a voluntary system?

Mr. MARTIN. Well, I would like to emphasize, and I hope you do understand that you can take those States on those charts—Arkansas, Alabama, Louisiana, Tennessee, Kentucky, Indiana, non-participating States. As long as those arrest cards are being taken for that murder and forwarded to the FBI, the FBI is automating that record and making it available through Triple I. It is just simply that the FBI becomes the one giving that criminal history up rath-

86-004 O - 95 - 3

er than me going to Arkansas or Louisiana and getting it out of their State repository.

So the FBI is spending a lot of our tax dollars, by the way, in stepping in and filling that void for those non-participating States. But I firmly believe, though, that once a State steps forward and accepts those Triple I standards, there is a direct relationship with the whole quality record system in that State, and that is what needs to happen.

Senator DORGAN. But do we have circumstances where States say, "Yes, we participate, except we are not going to send the records in for a year or so after it happens?" So what has happened is you have circumstances out there that represent the evidence of crime, but it is not transmitted for a year. Is that now happening?

Mr. MARTIN. That is happening, and I will tell you something else that is happening in my State, I am sad to say, and embarrassed. We continue to expand the use of the uniform traffic ticket in my State, and all law enforcement knows what I am talking about here. That allows an individual to be charged with a criminal offense, given a ticket, and you are on your way, no bond hearing, and many times they are not subjected to the full booking process. We miss those fingerprints. We don't get them at arrest.

We come through adjudication. Very seldom is the person there to get those fingerprints. Triple I and our criminal records system are based on fingerprints. We are missing now thousands of arrests in South Carolina because of the lack of resources at the local level. They don't want to bring that officer out of the field any more than necessary in order to bring that person back to the station house to put him through the booking process.

So while we are trying to get better, more comprehensive, more timely, more accurate records, because of limited resources out there in local law enforcement we at the same time are losing criminal history record information.

Senator DORGAN. I understand that point. That also is important, I think, the issue of how many of these you lose. The other point I was trying to make is, and I don't have the information in front of me, but I understand that there are some states that have an enormous backlog and so the information doesn't get transmitted for a year, 1½, 2 years. If that is the case, then you don't have an accurate database, even though you have a participating State.

I also understand that it becomes a set of priorities out there. They say, "Well, what is important?" Well, what is important is to chase these people and throw them in jail. It is less important to spend the money to keep these records up-to-date, to keep shoveling the information into this computer system so that it is up-to-date, so that you can save a life someplace else. That is the issue, and we are going to confront this on the question of mandates. We are going to have a bill on the floor of the Senate in January that mayors and governors are pushing, which says, "We don't want any more mandates."

Well, the reason I raise this question here is, we have a voluntary system and I frankly think that if I hold a hearing 6 years from today in the year 2000, I think that we will have testimony in which people say, "We have made an enormous amount of progress, but we are not there yet." Why? Because this system relies on the voluntary cooperation and the determination that this is a priority in all of the reaches of local governments around this country in order to make it work.

Is that an unfair characterization, Mr. Krupo?

Mr. KRUPO. No, sir. It is right on it. You know, I am going out on a limb here, and I do this on occasion. A mandate might be what is needed. We are not real successful where we are. Everybody is struggling, everybody is trying the best they can, but the real issue—and I wish you had been in your position years ago when we talked about centralized data bases, distributed data bases, and all these things, and it is kind of a nightmare to administer this.

Right now, there is a very satisfactory methodology for reporting crimes. There is the uniform crime report. We don't have a mandate, but you had better get your statistics in in a certain format and show up in the book at the end of the year or you are in serious trouble. That same kind of mandate does not exist with Triple I.

When we started SEARCH, it was a good idea and we knew where we were going. Again, it is a matter of priorities and it is a matter of funding at the local level. I will give you my jurisdiction as an example. Our courts do a fine job. They are overworked, overburdened, and everything else, but they are a separate entity of government. Even the mayor in the District of Columbia cannot order the D.C. court to report dispositions to us. It is purely voluntary in nature.

Now, there are creative things that can be done with budgets and everything else to encourage them to do it, but I would submit that probably most of the law enforcement officials, if you surveyed them, are not afraid of a mandate. As a matter of fact, it might be welcome. I think most of the law enforcement guys on the front line that are participating in Triple I want it. I am waiting for the money to come to finish my 30-percent programming. We worked on the grant application last Friday, so I am kind of excited about it.

One thing—let me drift off—that is a tremendous asset now that we never envisioned in 1982 when we talked about this is the AFIS system, the automated fingerprint system. That is what the records are about. A name record is virtually worthless. It may be OK for some probable cause or letting me start to talk to somebody, but after that, absent the fingerprints, I don't have much. So there needs to be a big drive at the same time, and they are included in Triple I. The automated fingerprint side of it is critical and that is part of what we are making sure—that has slowed down—it has helped, but it has also slowed down the development a little bit because we hit with that system probably about 6 years ago before it really became popular with most of the States.

We get 30 cold hits a month on our AFIS system here in the city. We close cases in Arlington, Alexandria, Fairfax, P.G. on cold murder cases based on one fingerprint. When we start sharing that Nationwide through Triple I and through the FBI NCIC 2000, that is when we are going to see the big change. So, Senator, we are working on it.

Senator DORGAN. Well, you know, I spent 1 day about a year ago sitting down at the D.C. Superior Court system just because I kind of wanted to get a sense of what is happening in an inner city court system. I came away from that experience, just sitting and watching, thinking that the system is absolutely overwhelmed, just overwhelmed.

When you take a look at the records of the people that move in and out of this system through the revolving door, you get an even greater sense that we know who these people are. Most of them have long, long, long records. We need to protect law enforcement officers, we need to protect victims, we need to protect the whole system, and one way to do that is to keep track of who they are and where they are and what they have done.

I don't intend ever to oversimplify the job. It is not simple. You have got so many different ways of characterizing the same felony, one way in Louisiana, another way in Wyoming. The same crime is called something different. These things make it complex, so I don't want to oversimplify it, nor do I want to understate the importance of it. This is critically important and, frankly, it is not paid much attention by people who should all across this country.

Mr. Davis, for full disclosure purposes I should point out that I was appointed to the Advisory Commission on Intergovernmental Relations by the Majority Leader of the Senate a year or so ago and have raised this subject on their agenda. I look forward to the participation of ACIR on this issue because it is a uniquely capable organization of bringing together mayors, governors, members of the Congress, and others to figure out how we get through the eye of the needle here and get to where we want to go. The way we are going to save lives is to get to the finish line, and the quicker we get there, the better.

I want to thank the three of you for presenting testimony. Some of the follow-up discussion to this testimony will occur in the next panel. Again, I want to say thank you very much for being with us.

The next panel represents several Federal officials who are involved in the Triple I. If you would please come forward. Mr. Steven Pomerantz is Assistant Director of the Federal Bureau of Investigation, accompanied by Mr. Emmet Rathburn, National Crime Information Center, the NCIC, in the FBI. Mr. Patrick J. Doyle is Chairman of the National Crime Information Center Advisory Policy Board.

Mr. Pomerantz, Mr. Rathburn, Mr. Doyle, thank you for being with us. You have heard some of the discussion, some of my comments, and the testimony, and I would appreciate receiving your testimony. I would say to you that we will include your entire testimony as part of the record. You are welcome to summarize it.

Why don't you proceed, Mr. Pomerantz, in whatever manner you choose?

TESTIMONY OF STEVEN L. POMERANTZ,[1] ASSISTANT DIRECTOR, FEDERAL BUREAU OF INVESTIGATION; ACCOMPANIED BY EMMET RATHBURN, NATIONAL CRIME INFORMATION CENTER

Mr. POMERANTZ. Thank you, Senator. I would like to summarize, if not read, this testimony because I think there have been so many issues raised this morning, so many very good issues, that I think the presentation set out in my statement is probably the most orderly way to approach the subject, and I think I will try to stop along the way and give some emphasis to certain areas based on what has been previously discussed here this morning.

The FBI began collecting criminal fingerprint and charge and disposition information in 1924, a very long time ago. Typically, when an offender is arrested in the United States, fingerprint cards are taken from that individual and used to identify the person, as well as to document the criminal offense charged at the time of arrest. Most arresting agencies mail the fingerprint cards to their State identification bureau, which sends one to the FBI for processing. A few large agencies are transmitting fingerprints electronically to the States, and I am going to discuss that later because it was mentioned earlier in testimony and I think it is very important.

These cards are the foundation and the basis for establishing State and national criminal history records. Positive fingerprint identification is critical to link subsequent arrests with the same individual, especially when that individual has assumed another name or has changed his or her identity in some way, which is an extraordinarily common occurrence in the criminal community these days.

Today, the FBI criminal identification files reflect records on about 32 million people who have been arrested and/or convicted of a criminal offense in the United States. For their mutual benefit, State and local arresting agencies throughout the country are encouraged to submit arrest fingerprint cards to the FBI for all criteria offenses; that is, all felony and all misdemeanor crimes except those designated as non-serious.

Senator DORGAN. And how many of them now do that?

Mr. POMERANTZ. The vast majority do that. We estimate that about 80 percent of the arrests that occur in the United States today are submitted, and some of those fall out, of course, because they are non-serious and for other reasons. The vast majority of law enforcement agencies in this country today do this.

Additionally, the FBI accepts final disposition and correctional information relating to those arrests. It is important to note that both fingerprint card submission and disposition reporting to the FBI, as has been stated many times today, is voluntary and the incidence and quality of reporting does vary from State to State.

Arrest reporting to the FBI is believed to be good in most States. Each day, we received between 18,000 and 20,000, and some days more, criminal arrest fingerprint cards. Historically, the——

Senator DORGAN. Excuse me for interrupting you, but can I just focus on that a little more?

[1] The prepared statement of Mr. Pomerantz appears on page 54.

Mr. POMERANTZ. Yes, sir.

Senator DORGAN. When you say it is good, are we talking 75 percent, 80 percent?

Mr. POMERANTZ. It is very difficult, given the number of law enforcement agencies and the number of arrests, to get an absolute handle on that question, but somewhere in the neighborhood of greater than 70, 75 percent, somewhere in excess of 80 percent.

The FBI historically has received disposition information for only about 50 percent of the reported offenses. Therefore, the FBI record would not always indicate whether or not a charge resulted in a finding of guilt, acquittal, or dismissal. More recently, we have automated the submission of disposition information to the extent that 17 States now submit this data to us using electronic media. These 17 States, more importantly, comprise 81 percent of all dispositions submitted to the FBI.

Senator you have indicated an interest in the Triple I, a very strong interest. I would like to provide you with a brief description of that program and the status of how it is operating today in support of the criminal justice community.

You may recall that I mentioned earlier the fact that at the time of arrest, one set of arrest fingerprints is routinely submitted to the State identification bureau in the State where the person is arrested. All States have such a bureau operating today, although some are certainly more advanced than others. Also, many States have laws that require the reporting of both arrests and dispositions to the State. Because of this, in many States the State's records will contain information that was not reported to the FBI.

In an effort to work toward a decentralized system, a little over 10 years ago, as we have heard earlier, we began working with State program officials to establish the Triple I. The Triple I was developed through a series of operational phases to computerize the interstate exchange of criminal history records. This was done using only existing resources and budgets both at the national level and the State level.

The FBI role in the Triple I is to maintain a fingerprint index for the record of each offender, a computerized name index for these records, and a pointer to the State holding the details of the arrest and disposition. Also, the FBI maintains the records of persons arrested for Federal offenses. Authorized criminal justice agencies may make inquiry of the Triple I name index from computer terminals connected to the NCIC system.

A second communications network, the NLETS, is used by the States to return and exchange the records among themselves. Twenty-nine States currently have their computerized files, as we have heard earlier, interfaced with the Triple I. We expect that at least 5 additional States will join the program next year; about 5 others are in the active system design phase, and the remaining 11 States and the District of Columbia were conducting planning activities when we canvassed the States earlier this year. A listing of the 29 States is available and you have also got it, sir, on the map.

These States who are participating today represent about 75 percent of the population and more than 80 percent of the arrests in the country today. Perhaps the most important point I can make in light of previous testimony I'll make now. The FBI provides its computerized records for the 21 States who have not interfaced their computers with the Triple I, and we also provide the records of Federal offenders. Thus, 100 percent of the records on persons with an automated FBI record are readily available for criminal justice use nationwide.

If you will allow me a moment to elaborate on that, what we are saying here is that although a State is not active and not a full participant in the Triple I, when we receive those arrest record cards from those 19 States we update the Triple I. So it is not as if those records from those 19 States do not get into the Triple I; they do.

Senator DORGAN. Well, I think it is easier for me probably to ask some questions as we go along.

Mr. POMERANTZ. Yes, sir.

Senator DORGAN. That solves the problem to the extent that you don't have a delay in the submission. I would like to ask you about how quickly are these records being submitted to you and, second, the implication of that would be to say that 100 percent of the records are readily available. The records of 20.5 million offenders were indexed in Triple I. That is not necessarily a substitute for saying complete records.

Mr. POMERANTZ. No, it is not.

Senator DORGAN. Records are different than complete records. You might have fragments of records. Second, the records you do have may be submitted today for an arrest 9 months or a year ago.

Mr. POMERANTZ. All of those things are certainly true, sir. The point I think I am making here is that is true whether or not the State is a Triple I State or whether we are entering its records on behalf of those 19 now non-participating States. But, certainly, what you say is accurate.

Senator DORGAN. I understand your point. The point you are making is the fact that we list a State that is not participating doesn't mean there aren't some records involved and some exchanges of information. By the same token, the fact that you are keeping automated records of arrests and fingerprints, and so on, from those States doesn't mean that you have complete records, nor does it mean that the records are submitted to you in a timely way.

Mr. POMERANTZ. Yes, sir, accurate on all counts. In a similar fashion, the same things could be said about those states that are participating in Triple I.

Senator DORGAN. I am going to get to that. Yes, I understand that point and that is the other question. That gets back to the question of will and priority. Is there a will to do this, to say that this is a priority, this is urgent, we need to do this, we are going to save lives? Or is it kind of the backwater of law enforcement duties? You say, "Well, our priority is going out there and chasing somebody today that committed a crime today, not trying to dust off some records on somebody that we apprehended and arrested and put in jail 3 months ago and ship them to Washington."

Mr. POMERANTZ. I would not argue with that characterization at all; no, sir, I wouldn't.

Senator DORGAN. Why don't you proceed?

Mr. POMERANTZ. Yes, sir. From the beginning, the Triple I was primarily intended to be used by criminal justice agencies for criminal justice purposes. More recently, however, with the enactment of the Brady Handgun Violence Prevention Act in November 1993 and other State legislation regulating firearms sales, the Triple I has taken on a new workload.

Each week, we record the number of transactions processed by the system and examine them according to the purpose for which they were made. During October of this year, for example, the Triple I processed 2.9 million inquiry and record request transactions for local, State, and Federal user agencies. More than 2.2 million of these were inquiry transactions of the index. 350,000 of these were for firearms-related checks; 1.9 million were for miscellaneous criminal justice purposes. Again, there is a chart attached, sir, that will give you more detail about the transactions.

System response times, as you have heard earlier, are very rapid. In fact, many agencies have reported to us that the information they receive from NCIC and the Triple I records are among the most valuable investigative tools that they have.

Senator I would like to expand on my comments earlier about the prior and current funding, if I might for a moment, for the Triple I program. I made the comment that the Triple I was developed over the years using existing systems and with no funding specifically earmarked for this purpose.

Senator DORGAN. Let me just interrupt one more time, and I apologize for that. Let me go back to the previous paragraph on page 5. You skipped over that, and I wanted to just touch base on it.

Mr. POMERANTZ. Yes, sir.

Senator DORGAN. You talked about the State of Virginia. Gun dealers place telephone calls to the State Police and provide information on pending gun sales. I am assuming, and I don't know anything about this, but I am assuming that in Virginia if one wants to purchase a handgun, they have a requirement, an instant records check. Is that right?

Mr. POMERANTZ. That is correct, sir.

Senator DORGAN. And they are checking with a record that is in a repository in Virginia and also they are probably checking with the records in the Triple I?

Mr. POMERANTZ. That is correct, sir, yes.

Senator DORGAN. And if I am a convicted felon who committed a crime somewhere in this country within the last 6 or 8 years, or committed 6 different felonies in different States, how likely is it that I am going to be accessed in these files?

Mr. POMERANTZ. Senator, I could not give you a specific answer as to exactly how likely it would be. I can again tell you that we have 20 million individuals indexed in Triple I, but I couldn't give you any precise answer on exactly how likely that was.

Senator DORGAN. The reason I asked the question is I think it is useful. I think an instant records check makes a lot of sense for not just handgun purchases, but for all gun purchases. An instant records check is supported by virtually everybody, including the NRA. But an instant records check prevents previously convicted felons from getting guns only if the record is complete.

Mr. POMERANTZ. Yes, sir.

Senator DORGAN. And if you have incomplete records, then the records check gives you a false sense of security.

Why don't you proceed?

Mr. POMERANTZ. Yes, sir. While the statements about the funding were true for the development of the system, the FBI did receive $10 million in fiscal year 1994 for purposes of the Brady Act, of which about $7.4 million is being used to upgrade the computer hardware to support the additional inquiries being made of Triple I for firearms-related purposes. $27 million in Federal funds were made available previously to the States through the Bureau of Justice Statistics to flag the records of convicted felons and to otherwise improve their criminal history capabilities.

With the passage of the crime bill in September of 1994, an additional $100 million was appropriated primarily for Brady Act purposes, of which the FBI will receive $6 million to begin establishing the national instant criminal background check system. About $88 million of the remaining money will go to State and local agencies to improve their record systems and their ability to make firearm-related background checks.

We have begun our study on how the national instant criminal background check system, which we call NICS, will function. We are working on this with a task group of State and local criminal justice officials and with Federal agency representatives. It appears that the Triple I will be the backbone of the NICS, which is intended to provide a broad range of information on persons who are disqualified from possessing firearms.

In addition to containing data on disqualifying criminal convictions, the NICS will contain other information, for example, on persons dishonorably discharged from the armed forces, persons who have been committed to mental institutions, as well as those who are under a court order restraining them from harassing, stalking, or threatening their spouse or other intimate partner.

Under the Brady Act, the Attorney General is to have the NICS operational by November of 1998. We are not far enough along at this time in analyzing the system's requirements to tell you what additional funding will be needed to complete the system and get it fully operational.

The Triple I, the NICS, and how these systems are accessed by tens of thousands of computer terminals throughout the country entails some details which are not easily described. I would like to make it clear, however, at this point that the Triple I I have been describing involves record inquiries and record requests that usually are based on a person's name, data of birth, sex, and race. These are the basic data elements that constitute most inquiries.

The submission of fingerprints for searching criminal files, however, remains the most thorough and the only positive means of determining whether or not a record exists for an individual, and I would like again to emphasize that, sir. That is the single biggest weakness of any system that we might discuss, regardless of its completeness or accuracy, and that has been, I think, testified to over and over again this morning. I just would emphasize that point, that that is a name check system and as a name check system, that is its most substantial weakness, in my opinion.

In this regard, the FBI's Criminal Information Services Division has undertaken a several-hundred-million-dollar project that we refer to as the Integrated Automated Fingerprint Identification System, or IAFIS. When it is completed in 1998, IAFIS will have the capability of receiving fingerprints in an electronic format from a law enforcement agency, processing the fingerprints against a database of more than 30 million—in other words, against our entire criminal history database—and providing either a record or a no-record response back to the arresting agency while the offender is still in custody in about 2 hours.

We have contracted with three separate vendors to develop prototypes of the computer technology necessary for the AFIS portion of the system. From these three, we will select a single vendor in November of next year to build and install the full-blown operational AFIS. Although much of the information concerning this effort is procurement-sensitive, I would like to let you know that we are very excited and optimistic that this initiative is going to revolutionize the identification of criminals and the speed and accuracy with which these people are identified on an interstate basis.

In closing, sir, I would like to sincerely thank you for your interest in these law enforcement efforts, particularly those efforts to provide complete and timely criminal history information, because you are so right. That is an absolutely necessity for effective law enforcement in this country. I would be happy to answer any questions that you may have, sir.

Senator DORGAN. I have a couple of questions, Mr. Pomerantz, but let me hear next, and finally, from Mr. Patrick J. Doyle, who is Chairman of the NCIC Policy Advisory Board.

Mr. Doyle, your entire statement will be made part of the record and you may summarize.

TESTIMONY OF PATRICK J. DOYLE,[1] FLORIDA DEPARTMENT OF LAW ENFORCEMENT, AND CHAIRMAN, NATIONAL CRIME INFORMATION CENTER ADVISORY POLICY BOARD

Mr. DOYLE. Thank you very much, Senator. First, I would like to thank you and praise you for having this hearing. I think it is long overdue and I am very proud that you have taken the gauntlet and are really trying to do something about this.

Secondly, I want to give a disclaimer here. I see I am listed under Federal officials. I am very proud to tell you, sir, I am not a Federal official. I am with the State of Florida and I work for a living, so I am very proud of that fact and I would like to be sure of that disclaimer.

Senator DORGAN. You may be apprehended momentarily by that fellow on your left.

Mr. POMERANTZ. I have had to live with him for the last year as the Chairman of APB, sir, and I am accustomed to it.

Mr. DOYLE. Sir, with your permission, I would like to deviate from my prepared remarks. They obviously can be read into the record, and I would like to, I think, try as succinctly as I can to talk to a number of the issues that came up today.

[1] The prepared statement of Mr. Doyle appears on page 83.

I am proud to tell you that I have been in law enforcement since 1968. I was with the Palm Beach County Sheriff's Office driving a patrol car when I started. We would call in for criminal records checks. We called them CCH's in that time, and I was 21 and I thought, golly, I can make a call on my radio here and get all this mass of information from all over the world.

I then went to the police academy and found out I didn't really get it from the whole world, but I got it only from the Nation. The longer I lived in that world, the more I realized the best that ever happened to me in 1968 through 1970 was I was getting it from 13 States. We then went on and proceeded and everybody got a little disgruntled, so we went from 1974 until about 1979 down to 6 States. So when you called in for a criminal history record check alongside the road at 3:00 in the morning, you were really checking 6 State files.

I am very pleased and very proud to reiterate what I think a number of enforcement officials here today have said. Triple I is alive and well. I now can very safely tell you both as the keeper of the records and the collector of the records for over 12 years, and now back on the street as the special agent in charge of a massive unit in the State of Florida, that I can safely say that when I call for a criminal record check, I am getting a 100-percent check of all States. That is not a 100-percent perfect database; it is not.

Major Martin mentioned the fact of the summons; that is a major issue. The FBI had a needed reject policy for a lot of years. We lost records there. Sometimes, Florida included, States just don't get their records in in a quick, timely fashion. We all need to. I haven't heard of any delays of a year to 2 years in any massive form. I am sure things do drop through the cracks when you are dealing with this amount of record, and we are dealing with millions and millions of records.

I am here to tell you today, sir, that I am proud of the system. It is growing, it is growing well. The other states that are not participants need to be, but they need to be not so that we can get the records that they are already sending in and we are already getting. We need to be able to get to those insignificant arrests that do occur that don't get in; that is, if you query Florida, we may only have one record at the national level in Triple I, but if you then transferred to Florida where you will get our full record, you will get our full, complete record; that is to say, if you are not wearing a shirt on the sidewalk in the town of Palm Beach and you are arrested there, that is an insignificant charge that at the Federal level shouldn't go, but we do keep that at the State level and you will get that record, also.

So by virtue of Triple I, you are getting a more complete, accurate record because all the records that Mr. Pomerantz has alluded to that don't go in, when a Triple I participant responds to a record, you are getting all the record that they have in that State, given it was inputted.

The other thing we have been talking about today is Triple I, and we saw the video and I know John Walsh from a lot of years ago, just a great guy. I mean, his head, his heart, and his motives are in such the right place that I am very gratified to call him a Floridian, also.

In looking at that, we are really not talking about who gave the criminal histories and who didn't. We are really talking about positive identification. That is the major fallacy in the whole criminal justice system, is lack of positive identification. Mr. Pomerantz talked about IAFIS, and Mr. Martin. We all mentioned IAFIS. I think there needs to be a major hearing on the Integrated Automated Fingerprint Identification System. That is, to law enforcement's perspective today, the only positive means of identification that is readily acceptable and readily available to the man on the street.

Under NCIC 2000, the Harris Corporation has developed, along with the FBI and the home office, as a matter of fact, in Great Britain, a good algorithm where you can walk up to a car tetherless and say, put your finger on here, Bud, and you can transfer back to the wanted files in Washington and find out—regardless of what this fellow says his name is, find out who he is and what he has done.

We are still a little off on that and that is a very expensive proposition, but the FBI, the Senate, and the House of Representatives of this Nation have bitten the bullet to date in helping to fund that. We need to continue that funding. That is critical, and that, in fact, will help to stop and solve the problem of lack of positive identification in this Nation. That is what we are really here talking about today. Participation is important in Triple I, but it is not the most important thing.

The arrest reports are going in, not every single one and not every one in a timely manner, but they are going in. As long as I know there is an arrest, I can get a disposition. As long as I know there is an arrest, I can call that agency and get the MO off the arrest report or the case investigative report and help determine am I working a serial killer.

I think we need to talk a lot more at the Senate level, particularly in your Committee, sir, and you certainly have an interest, about IAFIS, about VCAP, the Violent Crime Apprehension Program the FBI sponsors, woefully underfunded. We talk about nonparticipants. I don't know anybody in this day and age that even participates because it is so cumbersome because we haven't been able to keep up with time.

Lastly, with regard to the items that I think we should be talking about, there are a number of things on the horizon. In Florida, we are the first in a lot of things. We are the first in Triple I, the first missing children clearinghouse, the first with a missing persons file. We were first in most everything. Hearing this hearing today and listening to some of your comments, I think Florida is the greatest State, but I think North Dakota certainly is growing close with the representation they have from you.

But I do think States—Florida, for an example—are developing applications, investigative applications, that can help stem the tide of violent crime, which is what we all need to be about. VCIS is what we call in Florida the Violent Crime Information System. It takes MO data, not even fingerprints, but MO data—what did the guy do at a vicious crime; of the 88 different data elements we collect, what did he do—and compares them.

We just linked 5 murders in Florida together. They all had the same perpetrator and we didn't know it. They had been committed over 2 years. Now, we know who the gentlemen is. Luckily, he was arrested in Connecticut, but we didn't even know we were working the same crimes. You talk about law enforcement not sharing information. I don't think it is because law enforcement doesn't want to all the time. I think it is a lot of times they don't know where to go and how to do it.

But by creating and funding through grant programs innovative approaches to combatting violent crime, by properly funding and keeping the heat on Triple I, certainly IAFIS has got to happen in this Nation if we are ever going to have positive identification from the patrol car to the Nation's Capital, the central repositories. All those things have to be funded and we have to keep the light on them, if you will, and it is through people like you that we do that.

I think today I listened a lot about Triple I and I thought, boy, we are beating something that is really great. The fact of the matter is I don't think we are beating it up. It is good, it is working. We need more participation, but we are getting criminal histories. We are getting those we need. No, we are not getting every one and, no, they are not complete. Out of that $27 million, Florida has had about $1.2 million. We have increased our disposition reporting level from 46 percent to 69 percent. It doesn't sound like much, but we have a database of 2.2 million felonies in the State, people with different records in the State, so we are certainly putting that money to good use.

The $88 million that Steve spoke of earlier will certainly be helpful to all the States, also, but it is far more than one system; it is far more than Triple I. We need to talk about the basis of all these systems, and that is positive identification and other kinds of applications that can help identify a serial killer as he is out there doing the serial tasks that he is doing, not necessarily—normally, once they are arrested and we find out, oh, gee, he did 3 murders, they are not going back to the street. It is too late then. We need to be able to identify that there is a serial crime going on and then work it from there jointly with who did that crime.

So I think you are to be applauded again, sir, and I am very proud to be invited here.

Senator DORGAN. Well, Mr. Doyle, thank you for coming and bragging about Florida. We appreciate the fact that you have obviously been charged by the Chamber for spreading goodwill. We appreciate your coming here to testify.

Mr. Rathburn, did you have anything to add, or has Mr. Pomerantz——

Mr. RATHBURN. Mr. Pomerantz did an excellent job.

Senator DORGAN. I will be the judge of that. [Laughter.]

Mr. POMERANTZ. He works for me, Senator.

Senator DORGAN. I can tell.

Mr. Pomerantz, let me ask you if we can get from you some guide posts here. I should say in response to Mr. Doyle it is not my intention to beat up on the Triple I, but the first time I became interested in this and asked the question, the response from the FBI and Justice and others, including some on my staff who evaluated it or looked at it, was "Boy, we are pretty much complete here, we are headed in the right direction."

I looked at that information and I said, "You know, that doesn't sound right to me." I mean, I am not saying we haven't accomplished some things and I am not saying some people aren't working hard, but it seems to me we are a long way from home base on the question of whether we are establishing an accurate, up-to-date list of the records of felons in this country. The more I looked into it—I described a meeting I had in my office—the more I became convinced that this is a system that relies on voluntary cooperation and, at the moment, we are still some long way from having the kinds of records that are necessary.

What should we look for? In other words, what would the plan be by the FBI and the Justice Department to have in place by next year, the year after, 3 years, 5 years—do you have some guide posts by which we can measure whether or not we are getting there? What is the end date? What are some things for us to look at along the way? Is there a central plan?

Mr. POMERANTZ. That is a difficult question, sir. I wasn't around in this business—certainly, in the FBI, but not in this end of it when Triple I was conceived and the original operating plans were put into effect. I am told, however, that for a variety of reasons, because it is a voluntary system, many of the things you have heard—because there was never any funding for it, particularly at the State and local level, there were never any goals established in terms of numbers of States by a certain time, nor do we have those kinds of milestones at this point in time.

We know, for example, that of the known arrests in this country, we are getting about 80 percent of those each year onto Triple I. The other 20 percent, the best that we can prognosticate, is not necessarily that they are being missed in the sense that they should be on a system. There are a number of them that don't meet the level.

However, let me try to answer your question this way. I think one of the things that has occurred, and it has been alluded to, again, several times, that is going to move this along much more rapidly is what Congress did in terms of the Brady Act. It may be, in a way, an incidental consequence of that, but because money was made available and because time limits were set for the implementation of that Act and because we must respond to that statutory requirement, probably a consequence of that is going to be a more rapid implementation because the States will be spending that money to bring their systems up to the level that they need to be to join Triple I.

Senator DORGAN. But I understand that when we had $27 million available, they had difficulty finding grants to fund to spend the $27 million in upgrading these programs. If that were the case, that represents to me that there is a lack of will out there, and coming in now with $100 million is not going to solve the problem in a voluntary system unless there is a will out there that says this is a priority.

Mr. POMERANTZ. I would say a couple of things. First of all, sir, I was not involved, again, in this business so I cannot comment. I have no knowledge—it is not that I can't comment; I just don't have the knowledge of that $27 million, besides which those grants, as you probably are aware, are administered by the Bureau of Justice Statistics. We really have no input into that.

I will say that certainly I think P.J. did a good job in summarizing it, but the significance that I think law enforcement is attaching to all of these issues of criminal histories and criminal identification and criminal history recordkeeping has intensified and is continuing to intensify, for a whole variety of reasons. The mobility of criminals, the emphasis on the serial killers, the knowledge that has come to law enforcement through those investigations of the interstate nature of some of these people—all of that is focusing attention.

But you are also right, sir, when you talk about the fact that this is not the glamorous end of law enforcement, and that is a real issue. It does come down to resources and priorities. Which are you going to spend your money on, upgrading your criminal history recordkeeping capability, or putting more patrol cars out on the street, or a drug demand reduction program, or the whole host of other things that law enforcement has to deal with? You are correct. This frequently doesn't make the top of the list.

Senator DORGAN. Do you agree that it is not now an urgent national priority to complete a Triple I system that has accurate, up-to-date, and complete records with all States participating?

Mr. POMERANTZ. I have great difficulty answering that question on a national basis. I will say that for the Federal Government, particularly the FBI today, with the money we are spending on the IAFIS system, which is a little different aspect of this, but certainly in the same general area of criminal identification—and P.J. did a good job, also, of describing that—we are spending $500 million on that technology and another $200 to $300 million on the physical plant and the move to West Virginia. That is the biggest single dollar project the FBI has ever undertaken, so we certainly recognize the importance of this project.

I would say that by the money that is being expended in the States and the number of states that have come on, and particularly, as you can see from the map, the bigger States, the more populous states that account for 80 percent of the arrests of this country every year—given the tug at that available money to do all the variety of things that law enforcement has to do, I would say there certainly is an emphasis. I guess it is a question of how much and how soon.

Senator DORGAN. Let me answer the question I asked from my perspective. From my perspective, there is not any kind of an urgent priority that this get done. It is now a system in which the FBI and others have done commendable work to try to link a common database in all of the jurisdictions in the country and, on a voluntary basis, solicit cooperation. The payment to them for their cooperation is to not only require them to send information. The benefit is to allow them to access information. So they have a cost and they have a benefit.

It is totally voluntary and has progressed, in my judgment, more slowly than it would have progressed because it is voluntary. The question is: Will we ever get to the finish line under these circumstances? I am not sure I know the answer to that at this point and that is what concerns me.

Mr. Doyle, one of the interests I have, in addition to saving lives—making it so a police officer can apprehend someone some evening and be able to immediately access some database that shows that this person has committed 3 felonies in the last 8 months and is dangerous, so we know who he is, arrest him—in addition, it seems to me that having an accurate file of information also would persuade judges when sentencing to say, "This person has just been convicted. I now have in front of me the sheet. This sheet shows that this person has committed 12 felonies in the last 6 years. It is now time for me to say to this person, so long, we are not going to be seeing you for a while. You are a career criminal, you deserve to be off the streets. I am slapping you with a maximum sentence. You are going to spend a lot of time behind bars."

The absence of this sheet means that a judge is sitting there looking at that criminal for that offense and saying, "Well, you got a haircut and you got a blue suit now and you look pretty good to me, and this offense in itself, yes, was serious, and I will sentence you to this particular sentence as a result of what I now know." I want the judge to have this sheet, so the judge can say, "I don't care what color suit you have got on. I don't care when you got a haircut. You are a violent criminal and you are going to be gone for a long, long time." That is the import of this, as well, and I think unless it is complete and accurate and has the participation of all the States, you will never get to that point of helping judges during sentencing.

Mr. DOYLE. Sir, I certainly subscribe to that. However, Florida has sentencing guidelines, as do most States nowadays, and criminal histories are used for a myriad of reasons. Sentencing certainly is one. I guess where I really come at this thing is disposition reporting is important. Complete, extensive, accurate records are very important.

I feel very comfortable in telling you and telling my constituency in Florida, which is the law enforcement community, and telling that board, which is a national representation of the law enforcement community—telling them that I feel comfortable that we do a fairly good job on the arrest side. Steve was talking upwards of 80 percent of the arrests. I would venture to say it is closer—not 90, but probably closer to 90. I think that is pretty, pretty good, considering that in Florida we do about 3,000 arrests a day in Florida alone.

The issue you bring up is a very good one and that goes back again to a complete record, and that is the disposition reporting. A judge is never in this country going to sentence on an arrest or expand a sentence or call you a habitual offender on an arrest. They are going to do it on a conviction or on the disposition. That is where we are. Including Florida, we are all woefully inaccurate at this point—not inaccurate; we are inept. We are not anywhere close to 80, 90 percent, which is where we all need to be. I venture to say we will be getting there.

The $27 million, to go back to a question you asked earlier—I think there were a lot of reasons why that money didn't get spent, a lot of very poor reasons why that money didn't get spent for some people. For some, it was just it is not a big enough deal to write all that grant work.

Secondly, I would encourage you to encourage your colleagues over at the Bureau of Justice Statistics and the Bureau of Justice Administration to talk to the user people before they start publishing the guidelines. They publish them in the Federal Register and you have got 3 or 4 weeks to get a response in.

Senator DORGAN. Guidelines for what?

Mr. DOYLE. For grants, for all these granting programs. They want to give us money, but then they want to say, here is the money, you have got to do it our way, this way, and the way we say. That is what the guidelines basically do.

So I encourage this Congress to try to soften through President Clinton, I would imagine, the Justice Department, BJS, BJA, and let us help write those guidelines so we can do the things that they want done. Instead of being told how to do it, let us tell you how we are going to do them.

Lastly, in response to your question about how urgent is this, I think Triple I is important. I don't think it is urgent. I think what is urgent is in North Dakota today—I believe they do instant checks there—is when they make a phone call and somebody goes to a gun dealer in Florida or anywhere else in this Nation that I know, they are going up and saying, here is my driver's license or some photo I.D., and they are calling in name, race, sex, date of birth.

Now, doggone it, these bad guys are smart and they have been around. Our alias file at FDLE, the central repository, has over 300,000 aliases in it attached to those 2.2 million records I spoke of. Now, doggone it, those guys are smart enough to go get a phony I.D. and be John Dillinger. How is that gun dealer going to know the difference when he is calling that in, or how is your State law enforcement official going to know the difference when they are going—here is P.J. Doyle, white male, date of birth 10–10–10, when really I am John Dillinger and I just did the Friday the 13th massacre. Nobody is going to know that without positive identification. That is what this country has got to move to.

I think there are a lot of impediments. Technology and money are a minor part of it. I think it is a major attitude, also, but we have to get the positive identification. We were the first State in the Nation to have a total, comprehensive weapons program. We deny about 2 to 3 percent a year, over 333,000 every year.

Senator DORGAN. Excuse me for interrupting, but go back to the question of attitude. You just said it is not just technical and it is not just money. It is attitude. Tell me what you mean by that.

Mr. DOYLE. There are two pieces of attitude I would love to share with you. I am certainly glad you asked. These are a couple of my favorite stories. We do record checks for gun purchases; we have been doing them 4 years. We do over 333,000 a year. We do them in 3.5 minutes, on the average; that is, from when the call comes into us, answered, and response back, on the average, 3.5 minutes.

When I was the director of that division, I used to get at least three calls a week from citizens complaining that they didn't want to wait the 3.5 minutes to get that record checked. My solution was always, well, when you went to buy a refrigerator or a washing machine at Sears, how long did that take you? A hell of a lot longer than 3.5 minutes. So the attitude of our society is we want service and we want it now, but I want to be exempted from that.

Secondly, two nights ago I was standing in a public supermarket. It is the largest chain of supermarkets in the State of Florida, home-based in Lakeland, Florida. I was standing there and a lady wanted to cash a check, and the lady said, well, do you have a work phone? She says, well, I don't have to give you that, and just went into this tirade about how she wasn't going to give her anything. Now, worthless checks are a serious problem to Publix, and I am certain a serious problem in this Nation, not a violent problem, but a serious problem.

Well, the attitude of the lady was, look, I am here and if you want my business, you do it my way, as I say. I think that a lot of folks in our society have that attitude. I can't wait for the day when in Florida—and we will be the first ones on NCIC 2000; no question in my mind about that—we will walk up to the window and say, put your finger here. I am dying to see the response of our general citizens when you tell them, oh, we are doing a fingerprint check. I just can't hardly wait to see what that attitude is going to be like.

Senator DORGAN. For what?

Mr. DOYLE. I am sorry?

Senator DORGAN. A fingerprinting check for what?

Mr. DOYLE. Criminal history, wanted persons.

Senator DORGAN. Cashing a check?

Mr. DOYLE. That is not a bad idea either.

Senator DORGAN. Well, you are raising a point about civil liberties and I understand that point, and I understand that whenever you talk about computer records of criminals, a database of people who committed felonies, these things always get involved in the discussion. There are a lot of other reasons that some would want to use these indexes. Somebody wants to work in a child care center and you want to know whether this person has committed previous acts of child sexual abuse, for example, and has been convicted. So you can go through a whole litany of reasons that one would want to access information.

My own view is that those who are convicted of felonies in this country have little reason to complain that the rest of us who have not committed felonies want to keep their names and their records and access those names and records in a central repository for purposes of law enforcement. I think when you are convicted of a felony, you waive your right to say, "Look, it is none of the people's business what I have done in the past." The heck it is not our business.

You in law enforcement know this much better than I do, but we do have an epidemic of violent crime in our country, and we can have the FBI say, it is marginally down by 2 percent or 4 percent here or there, but the fact is we have a terrible violent crime problem in this country that leaves almost every American feeling at times unsafe, worrying about their personal security. We have to respond to that.

It is interesting, as I said earlier this morning, that we go through these machinations of debating a crime bill. The fact is most crime has nothing to do with the Federal Government. Most crime is dealt with at the State and local level. Ninety to ninety-five percent of the crime doesn't have anything to do with Federal law. So we can do cart wheels here in Congress and get tough and create different sentencing guidelines, but the fact is, it won't affect 95 percent of the criminal justice system.

So we have to be smarter and we have to think through a little more carefully exactly what gives us the edge on these folks that are committing the crimes. One of the things I think that gives us the edge is having a good identification system.

Now, I don't agree with your statement, Mr. Doyle, that the Triple I is not the most important thing. At this point, it is the most important element and we need to finish it. I don't disagree that in the longer term, technologically, a fingerprint identification system, AFIS or some other system, is going to be an enormous benefit to the law enforcement system because Mr. Pomerantz makes the point, and I think he is quite right, that, in a lot of cases, we are not dealing with people who are stupid. They are not going to walk in and say, "I would like to buy a .38 and my name is John Jones," knowing that if somebody checks John Jones they will find 6 previous felonies. They are going to give a bad name or a bad identification. Unless you have the electronic capability of fingerprinting and other things, you probably won't catch that.

Tell me, Mr. Pomerantz, what does it cost to go to a more high-tech approach to identification? AFIS, for example, in the long term will cost what?

Mr. POMERANTZ. Well, as I said, our AFIS system—to bring it up and to make it fully operational is going to be $500 million. That is what it is going to cost. Now, that is our IAFIS system which is going to integrate all the AFIS systems throughout the country, bring them all in line and compatible with our IAFIS system, and that is what our initial investment is.

May I say something, Senator, about what you——

Senator DORGAN. Sure.

Mr. POMERANTZ. I don't think I would take a position as strong as P.J.'s on which is the more significant element of what we are doing. It seems to me they are all compatible and all work together, but I would make a point to support him. On the videotape that we saw at the very beginning of the hearing you saw, in Florida, those individuals stopped along the highway.

Now, the way I interpreted that is one of those individuals was arrested based on an NCIC check done instantaneously from the patrol car. The second individual was released after an NCIC check. I presume from what I saw on that tape the reason was, and I heard the officer say it, that the person gave a fictitious name. That is why that person was released.

Next year, or certainly by 1996 when NCIC 2000 is operational, that police officer would have the capability to take that individual's right index finger and roll it on a screen right there in that car and would get a response that that person was indeed a wanted person. So, that certainly emphasizes in a very graphic way the significance of the fingerprint-based identification over a name-based inquiry. That would not have happened if we had NCIC 2000 today.

Senator DORGAN. I understand that. As I said, I think that technologically the ability to move in that direction is going to be very helpful in creating positive identifications.

Let me go to another question that, Mr. Doyle, you alluded to. My understanding is that, when you start to deal with complete records, including dispositions, the percentage of complete and accurate records in the Triple I is somewhere around 20 percent. Am I off? I mean, my understanding is that we are far from having complete records, and you are right that a judge is not going to take a look at an arrest sheet. When sentencing someone the judge is going to look at what kinds of conviction record this person has. We don't have nearly the kinds of dispositions in these records that would give us even 50-percent accuracy or completion of the records. Is that right?

Mr. DOYLE. I would agree. The percentages, sir, I am not sure of, but I can assure you it is low. I can assure you 20 percent wouldn't surprise me in the least. You are very right. We do have to get far more inventive, if you will, about creating people and money and dealing with that workload to get those in. That is very, very important.

Senator DORGAN. Mr. Rathburn or Mr. Pomerantz, is the 20 percent largely because of old dispositions, or are we finding better compliance with dispositions that are more recent—in the last 5 years, as an example—and if so, can you describe that for me?

Mr. POMERANTZ. Yes, sir, most assuredly, and more than that it has been the use of submitting dispositions electronically that has been a gigantic step forward. I think I testified, and I will check with Emmet to make sure I am being accurate, but about 80 percent of our arrest data now includes disposition, which is a tremendous improvement.

There have been some concerted efforts, yes, in individual States and on our part, as well, to go back and actively seek out disposition data, but I think the greater progress has been made as a result of the ability of the States, again, particularly the larger States—we just brought California up on line with the submission of electronic disposition data and that has really made the more dramatic difference.

Senator DORGAN. I am going to try to see if we can find some guide posts here because I would like to know where we expect to be 24 months from now, 48 months from now. Where should we be? It just is not satisfactory to me that 4 years from now we will say, "We have done our best and look at what additional things we have accomplished." Yes, that might be true, but if we are not in the age of computers keeping track of who has committed America's crimes and accessing them for law enforcement purposes, I will be unsatisfied.

I think the only way we are going to get there is to establish a plan and say that this plan represents a priority for this country. That has to do with all of the larger discussions that we have here about funding and mandates and other things. It does require, I think, the work of the ACIR. I would hope that the FBI and the Justice Department will work with the ACIR. I think they are perfect to try to blend the interests of the various levels of government that must cooperate in order to make this happen.

I want to thank all of you for attending this morning. We will follow up on this in the next year. I am intensely interested in seeing that we make progress, and your contribution this morning is very helpful. Mr. Klaas, we appreciate your being here, and others, including the folks from the District of Columbia. I also would like to thank Katherine Needham from my office, and Gordon Hamel, who have helped coordinate with you to put this hearing together.

This will be the first step in an attempt to try to provide some focus and put the spotlight on to see what is happening. I want this to work. I want it to work to save lives, and I want it to work so that judges can put career criminals who commit heinous and violent crimes behind bars and keep them there. Frankly, the only way that this can happen is if we understand who they are and what they have done and where they are. That requires adequate, complete, and full disclosure of the records available to the entire law enforcement community.

I thank all of you for your cooperation, and this hearing is adjourned.

[Whereupon, at 1:15 p.m., the Committee was adjourned.]

APPENDIX

PREPARED STATEMENT OF MAX J. KRUPO

I am Assistant Chief of Police Max Krupo, the Technical Services Officer of the Metropolitan Police Department for the District of Columbia. I am very pleased to have this opportunity to represent Chief of Police Fred Thomas on this very important issue surrounding our efforts to identify the new breed of mobile criminal who is praying on our communities throughout this Nation. Chief Thomas regrets that he was unavailable to attend this hearing.

Let me say at the outset that the Metropolitan Police Department fully supports the triple I program. We have been working towards the full implementation of all aspects of III. An unrelated ordinance and court ruling in the early stages of this project severely restricted the District of Columbia's participation. However, in 1989 with the help of our City Council and Congress, we were able to establish legislation that opened the way for full participation. Since that time, efforts have been underway to create a fully automated criminal records system within our jurisdiction.

This task has not been easy since it requires the complete cooperation of all of the criminal justice agencies within the District of Columbia to record and report their criminal records information to one central data base. Heretofore, each agency was able to maintain their own individual record systems. The systems were manual and in many cases contained outdated information. The triple I program has no room for inaccurate record keeping which could result in the loss of a person's constitutional rights. We in law enforcement are well aware of the sensitivity of data on repeat violent offenders and the implications of our failure to safeguard the data. Our standards for record keeping are far more stringent than for any other profession. We cannot tolerate the plus or minus 10 percent error rate which is acceptable in other industries or professions. Our systems must provide instantaneous information that is unquestionably accurate, while at the same time providing complete and positive identification of the subject of the record. Few if any other systems on this earth require that level of accuracy. We in law enforcement accept and understand the need for such a mandate. However in an era characterized by shrinking budgets and increasing demands for services, we are in a systems development battle. You may be assured that the completion of the triple I program is at the top of our list.

Development on the triple I program has been progressing and will continue to be developed with the greatest of effort. We expect that the Metropolitan Police Department will have established full membership of the triple I program by December of 1995.

On June 20th 1994 Attorney General Janet Reno directed a memorandum to the Mayor of the District of Columbia wherein she established minimum mandatory dates for compliance with the National Child Protection Act of 1993 and the Brady Handgun Violence Prevention Act. The dates established by the Attorney General were arrived at after consultation with the Metropolitan Police Department and are consistent with how fast we feel that an orderly transformation of our criminal records system can be accomplished. This type of cooperation between the Federal Government and the respective state agencies has been the norm for this process. And I can state that this spirit is what has made our other law enforcement information systems so successful.

However, it must be stated here that in the eyes of police officers there is a huge difference between a criminal arrest record and a complete criminal history. While our goal is to create an automated system where each record is complete with all available information from the courts, parole and corrections systems, I feel that we will not reach that stage for some time. However, we can and will reach an interim goal where at least criminal arrest information will be available for immediate law enforcement uses.

The value of preliminary arrest data cannot be overstated. Many times preliminary arrest information on a subject can make a difference as to the level of scrutiny that individual receives during the course of an investigation. Certainly, the individuals rights must be protected, and final dispositions are needed for longer term investigations and court sentencing, but the mere fact that an individual was arrested is generally in most jurisdictions a matter of public information already.

We in the Metropolitan Police Department are moving to complete a system whereby the much needed preliminary arrest information I have been speaking about can be provided to law enforcement personnel as required under the guidelines of triple I. We are in concert with and have received full support from the FBI in this project. Without their assistance we would not be as advanced as we are today.

As one of the original members of the Search Group who helped conceive this idea of a triple I, I can state that we envisioned a Cadillac of systems. We were advised by the technocrats at that time that every feature and capability we wanted was within our reach. However, I sit before you today, 10 years later, certain in the knowledge that there are many problems when you try to standardize automated systems. In hindsight, I think it's fair to say that we grossly underestimated the massive technical requirements needed to take this process from concept to reality. As time goes on and we continue development with current and future technology, these standardization problems will become a thing of the past. Given the direction of automated fingerprint systems in this nation, I feel confident that the days where a criminal could sneak through the system merely by changing his name and growing a beard have come to a close. In the future we will see imaging systems that allow law enforcement officers to positively identify suspects on the street from their patrol cars in partnership with technology.

In closing let me state for the record that while the development of this system has been agonizingly slow we have not been sitting on our hands. Since 1989 the Metropolitan Police Department alone has submitted approximately 80,000 criminal arrest records supported by fingerprints to the FBI for inclusion into the triple I system. The FBI has diligently worked with the MPD in this process and I am confident that our most serious criminals can, as a result, be located by other law enforcement agencies throughout the United States.

The MPD is currently classified as a participant in triple I, which means that we can make inquiries into the system and receive responses. However our records are not yet automated enough to allow us to be classified as full members and exchange information with other agencies through the automation of the triple I system. This problem is being addressed as we speak. Programmers are more than 70 percent complete in their efforts to create the necessary interfaces, data entry personnel are working tirelessly to convert 700,000 plus existing manual records into a computer readable format. And, booking officers are being trained to perform accurate data entries into this newly created system.

I fully expect that the MPD will meet the guidelines set forth in the previously specified legislation and those further defined by the Attorney General.

Thank you for the opportunity to appear before this body. I hope that my testimony has helped ease the concerns that any members may have had concerning the design and implementation of the most comprehensive information system ever developed for law enforcement.

I would be happy to answer any questions that the panel may have at this time.

PREPARED STATEMENT OF WILLIAM E. DAVIS

Mr. Chairman, my name is William Davis. I am the Executive Director of the U.S. Advisory Commission on Intergovernmental Relations (ACIR). I want to thank you for the opportunity to present comments on behalf of the ACIR and its Chairman, William F. Winter, regarding the Interstate Identification Index (III).

Mr. Chairman, as you are aware as one of the members representing the U.S. Senate on the ACIR, our Commission was established by the Congress in 1959 to monitor and recommend improvements to the American Federal System of Government This responsibility is very wide-ranging covering structural, policy, fiscal, regulatory, and legal relationships and impacts, as well as concerns for the effective and efficient performance of the Federal System.

Certainly the intergovernmental dimension of crime prevention and criminal justice are part of ACIR's focus and concern. ACIR's attention to criminal justice reaches back to the 1970's when the Commission published such works as *Making the Safe Streets Act Work: An Intergovernmental Challenge, State-Local Relations in the Criminal Justice System*, and *Safe Streets Reconsidered: The Block Experience*

(1968–1975). Additional studies were released in the 1980's and, as recently as 1993, ACIR published an extensive work on a *Guide to the Criminal Justice System for General Government Elected Officials.*

ACIR's attention to the issues surrounding the Interstate Identification Index was raised by yourself, Mr. Chairman, at a Commission meeting this year. At that meeting, our members heard from Kent Markus, Deputy Attorney General for the Department of Justice, on the importance, strengths and weaknesses of the triple III. As a result of this discussion, our Commission adopted as one of its work agenda items ACIR's efforts to help stimulate the full implementation of the triple III as well as the pace of this implementation by those states that had not as yet done so.

Since that Commission meeting, we have met with staff of the Department of Justice and FBI, as well as the National Governor's Association, to become better informed about the background of the triple III, its status with respect to implementation by the states, and to determine what steps that ACIR could take, in cooperation with organizations such as NGA, to help achieve the kind of National felon registry database that is of concern to leaders such as yourself, Mr. Chairman, and others.

Our background efforts, thus far Mr. Chairman, have confirmed in our minds the importance of the triple III to the national effort for combating crime and career criminals, which are responsible for a disproportionate percentage of all crimes as repeat offenders.

The tragic experience of the death of Mr. Klass's daughter, who was killed by a repeat offender even after he was earlier interviewed by local law enforcement officers for an unrelated incident and unaware of his past criminal background, is certainly a poignant example of the importance of the triple III. Had this information system been in place and fully functional, this tragic death may have been prevented. This tragedy was made much worse with the knowledge that we have the capacity to have prevented it if only that capacity had been used.

In a sense, therefore, the real tragedy is that only 29 states have elected to implement the triple III as of this date. And even with this number of states, of the approximate 50 million criminal records nationwide, the FBI's triple III database contains only about 18 million of those records and, of those, only about 9 million are complete records including court disposition of those cases.

This tragedy is made even worse because the Federal Government has provided funding assistance to the states to aid them for such purposes as the purchase of equipment, programming of software, and training of personnel to operate the system. Of the $27 million that was made available to the states for this purpose by the Anti-Drug Abuse Act of 1988, we found that a large proportion of this money has yet to be expended (or fully expended) by several states. The $100 million recently appropriated by the Brady Handgun Violence Prevention Act for improving state criminal record information systems has given some people renewed confidence that the states that have not yet implemented the triple III might do so in the future.

While the number of states that have implemented the triple III have continued to grow over the last few years, the total still is only slightly more than one-half of the states, and the pace of implementation continues to be very slow.

To date, Mr. Chairman, we are unaware of any research that has explained why some states are not participants in the triple III, or why records are late or incomplete. Some of the possible reasons that have been mentioned are:

- That some states lack the proper technology in the form of equipment, software compatibility, or training (a situation hard to understand with the availability of Federal assistance to meet these needs);
- That the implementation of the triple III is simply not a high priority in some state policy agendas. This view is often coupled with the suspicion that this lack of priority may be due to the fact that the relevant program staff responsible for such information systems have not elevated the policy issue to the Governor's attention sufficiently to achieve results;
- That there is simply not adequate understanding by some in the states of how the triple III can truly benefit law enforcement and criminal justice in those states, or that there is sufficient funding and technical assistance available to help in the implementation of the triple III;
- That the separation of the law enforcement and criminal justice functions in the states, between the state executive and judicial branches, causes problems of "turf", that in turn have inhibited cooperation in the sharing (or timely exchange) of data necessary for input to the state's central repository of criminal data and case disposition;

- And finally, there is the view that the lack of implementation may be a problem of local government understanding of the benefits (or use) of the triple III. In other words, if there were sufficient local government pressure to implement the triple III, there might be increased incentive for state action.

Mr. Chairman, ACIR has developed a preliminary set of objectives that we believe might be useful in helping to promote a fuller and more rapid implementation of the triple III. These objectives have been developed in cooperation with NGA, and we intend to include other national interests as well as we refine these objectives and actions related to those objectives. These objectives include:

- Determining with greater certainty the barriers or impediments for the slow pace of implementing the triple III. In order to undertake effective actions to stimulate state action, we need to be clear as to the problems that must be addressed;
- Second, we want to raise the visibility of the importance of the triple III, the assistance available for implementation, and the positive benefits of implementation; and
- Finally, we want to undertake actions that will encourage and stimulate implementation as a worthy investment of time and effort by the states.

Having adopted these objectives, the Commission asked the staff to develop a work plan for undertaking activities designed to achieve these goals. The actions below are the activities that have been proposed. However, ACIR's ability to carry-out each activity will depend on our finding additional assistance for these purposes. The activities proposed include:

- A survey of state and local officials to determine what the impediments are to the implementation of the triple III. The findings of this survey will help direct our remaining efforts including the dissemination of survey data as part of the effort to stimulate implementation of the triple III.
- Commission hearings around the country to raise the awareness of state and local officials of the triple III and its benefits. These hearings will be factfinding in nature to identify both the successes and failures of using or not using criminal record systems including triple III. In essence, these hearings will serve an educational purpose as well as information gathering one.
- Undertaking cooperative efforts with groups like NGA, NCSL, and others that involve workshops or presentations at conventions or other meetings of state and local officials for the purpose of promoting the triple III as well as serving as a information resource to answer the concerns of these officials;
- Utilizing ACIR's publications and those of other organizations to promote and provide information about triple III and the importance of implementation;
- Using other media sources to this same end, including print and electronic media to disseminate information intended to stimulate an interest in and actions leading to implementation.

Mr. Chairman, I can assure you that ACIR considers this issue to be extremely important and worthy of every effort to achieve full implementation throughout this nation. To the extent that our resources permit, we will certainly work to this end in cooperation with the intergovernmental community.

I want to thank you, Mr. Chairman, and this Committee for giving ACIR the opportunity to present these remarks today's. I shall be happy to answer your questions.

PREPARED STATEMENT OF STEVEN L. POMERANTZ

Mr. Chairman, thank you for the opportunity to appear before your Committee and provide this testimony about the FBI's role in identifying criminals and providing information about their prior criminal histories. Working with state program officials, we have accomplished a lot during the last 10 years to automate our data and we have plans to make vast improvements in the fingerprint identification process within the next several years.

The FBI began collecting criminal fingerprint and charge/disposition information for Federal and state arrests in 1924, which was the year Congress authorized the United States Attorney General to collect this information and exchange it with criminal justice officials. Typically, when an offender is arrested in the United States, arrest fingerprint cards are completed for the individual—to identify the person and to document the criminal offense charged at the time of arrest. Most arresting agencies mail the fingerprint cards to their state identification bureau which sends one to the FBI for processing. A few large agencies are transmitting fingerprints electronically to the states. These cards are the foundation and the basis for establishing state and national criminal history records. Positive fingerprint identification is critical to link subsequent arrests with the same individual, especially when that individual has assumed another name or has changed his or her identity in some way.

Today, the FBI criminal identification files reflect records on about 32 million people who have been arrested and/or convicted of a criminal offense in the United States. For their mutual benefit, state and local arresting agencies throughout the country are encouraged to submit arrest fingerprint cards to the FBI for all "criteria offenses", that is all felony and all misdemeanor crimes except those designated as non-serious ones. Additionally, the FBI accepts final disposition and correctional information relating to these arrests. It is important to note that both fingerprint card submission and disposition reporting to the FBI are voluntary and the incidence and quality of reporting varies from state to state. Arrest reporting to the FBI is thought to be good in most states. Each day, we receive between 18,000 to 20,000 criminal arrest fingerprint cards. Historically, the FBI has received disposition information for only about 50 percent of the reported arrests. Therefore, the FBI record would not always indicate whether or not a charge resulted in a finding of guilt, acquittal, or dismissal. More recently, I am happy to report, we have automated the submission of disposition information to the extent that 17 states now submit this data to us using electronic media. These 17 states, together, comprise 81 percent of all dispositions submitted to the FBI.

Your committee, through Senator Dorgan, has indicated its interest in the Interstate Identification Index program. I would like to provide you with a brief description of that program and the status of how it is operating today in support of the criminal justice community. You may recall that I mentioned earlier the fact that at the time of arrest, one set of arrest fingerprints is routinely submitted to the state identification bureau in the state where the person is arrested. All states have such a bureau operating today, although some are more advanced than others. Also, many states have laws that require the reporting of both arrests and dispositions to the state. Because of this, in many states, the state's records will contain information that was not reported to the FBI.

In an effort to work toward a decentralized system, a little over 10 years ago, we began working with state program officials to establish an Interstate Identification Index (Triple I) program. The Triple I was developed through a series of operational phases to computerize the interstate exchange of criminal history records. This was done using only existing resources and budgets within the states and the FBI. The FBI role in the Triple I is to maintain a fingerprint index for the record of each offender, a computerized name index for these records, and a "pointer" to the state holding the details of the arrest and disposition. Also, the FBI maintains records of persons arrested for federal offenses.

Authorized criminal justice agencies may make inquiry of the Triple I name index from computer terminals connected to the National Crime Information Center, otherwise known as the "NCIC". A second telecommunications network, the National Law Enforcement Telecommunications System, or "NLETS", is used by the states to return the detailed records. Twenty-nine states currently have their computerized files interfaced with the Triple I so that their computers can provide records for interstate criminal justice purposes. We expect that at least five additional states will join the program next year. about five others are in the "system design" phase, and the remaining 11 states and the District of Columbia were conducting planning activities when we contacted them earlier this year. A list of the 29 participating states is attached to my written statement. These states represent about 75 percent of the population and more than 80 percent of the arrests in the country. The FBI provides its computerized records for the 21 states who have not yet interfaced their computers with the Triple I, and also we provide the records of Federal offenders. Thus, 100 percent of the records on persons with an automated FBI record are readily available for criminal justice use nationwide. As of November 1st of this year, the records of 20.5 million offenders were indexed in Triple I.

From the beginning, the Triple I was primarily intended to be used by criminal justice agencies for criminal justice purposes. More recently, however, with the enactment of the Brady Handgun Violence Prevention Act, in November 1993, and other state legislation regulating firearms sales, the Triple I has taken on a new workload. Each week we record the number of transactions processed by the system and examine them according to the purpose for which they were made. During October of this year, the Triple I processed 2.9 million inquiry and record request transactions for local, State, and Federal user agencies. More than 2.2 million of these were inquiry transactions of the index. Three-hundred fifty thousand of these were for firearms related checks; 1.9 million were for miscellaneous criminal justice purposes such as bond hearings, risk assessment, and investigations. Please refer to the chart attached to my written statement for more details about these transactions.

System response times are rapid. In Virginia for instance, gun dealers place telephone calls to the state police and provide information on pending gun sales. Usually, they wait no longer than 1½ minutes while the state police check their files, the NCIC wanted person file, and the Triple I for any disqualifying information. In fact, many agencies have reported to us that the information they receive from NCIC and the criminal records they obtain through the Triple I are among their most valuable investigative tools.

Mr. Chairman, I would like to expand upon my comments about the prior and current funding for the Triple I program. Earlier in my opening remarks, I made the comment that the Triple I was developed over the years using existing systems and with no funding specially earmarked for this purpose. While this is true for the development of the system, the FBI did receive $10 million in fiscal year 1994 for purposes of the Brady Act, of which about $7.4 million is being used to upgrade the computer hardware to support the additional inquiries being made of Triple I for firearms related purposes. $27 million in Federal funds were made available previously to the states through the Bureau of Justice Statistics to flag the records of convicted felons and to otherwise improve their criminal history capabilities. With the passage of the crime bill, in September 1994, an additional $100 million was appropriated primarily for Brady Act purposes, of which the FBI will receive $6 million to start establishing the National Instant Criminal Background Check System. About $88 million of the remaining money will go to State and local agencies, as I understand it, to improve their record systems and their ability to make firearm related background checks.

We have begun our study on how the National Instant Criminal Background Check System which we call "NICS" will function. We are working on this with a task group of state and local criminal justice officials, and with Federal agency representatives. It appears that the Triple I will be the backbone of the NICS which is intended to provide a broad range of information on persons who are disqualified from possessing firearms. In addition to containing data on disqualifying criminal convictions, the NICS will contain other information, for example, on persons dishonorably discharged from the Armed Forces, persons who have been committed to mental institutions, as well as those who are under a court order restraining them from harassing, stalking, or threatening their spouse or other intimate partner. Under the Brady Act, the Attorney General is to have the NICS operational by November 1998. We are not far enough along at this time in analyzing the system's requirements to tell you what additional funding will be needed to complete this system and get it fully operational.

The Triple I, the NICS, and how these systems are accessed by tens of thousands of computer terminals throughout the country entails some details which are not easily described. I want to make it clear, however, at this point, the Triple I functions I have been describing involve record inquiries and record requests that usually are based on a person's name, date of birth, sex, and race. These are the basic data elements that constitute most inquiries. The submission of fingerprints for searching criminal files remains the most thorough and the only positive means of determining whether or not a record exists for an individual. In this regard, the FBI's Criminal Justice Information Services Division has undertaken a several hundred billion dollar project that we refer to as the "Integrated Automated Fingerprint Identification System", or IAFIS. When it is completed, several years from now, IAFIS will have the capability of receiving fingerprints in an electronic format from a law enforcement agency, processing the fingerprints against a data base of more than thirty million criminal history records, and providing either a record or a no record response back to the arresting agency, while the offender is still in custody perhaps as quickly as two hours. We have contracted with three separate vendors to develop prototypes of the computer technology necessary for the fingerprint identification portion of this process, known as the automated fingerprint identification system (AFIS). From these three, we will select a single vendor in November of next year to build and install the full-blown operational AFIS. Although much of the information concerning this effort is procurement sensitive and cannot be made public at this time, I would like to let you know that we are very excited and optimistic that this initiative is going to revolutionize the identification of criminals, and the speed and accuracy with which these people are identified on an interstate basis.

In closing, I would like to thank you for your interest in our law enforcement efforts, particularly those efforts to provide complete and timely criminal history information. Your support in these endeavors is greatly appreciated. I will be happy to address any questions you may have at this time.

Interstate Identification Index Program
State Participants/Record Providers

Alaska	New York
California	North Carolina
Colorado	North Dakota
Connecticut	Ohio
Delaware	Oklahoma
Florida	Oregon
Georgia	Pennsylvania
Idaho	South Carolina
Illinois	South Dakota
Michigan	Texas
Minnesota	Utah
Missouri	Virginia
Montana	Washington
Nevada	Wyoming
New Jersey	

Interstate Identification Index (Triple-I) Inquiry and Record Request Transactions

2,875,141 Transactions in October 1994

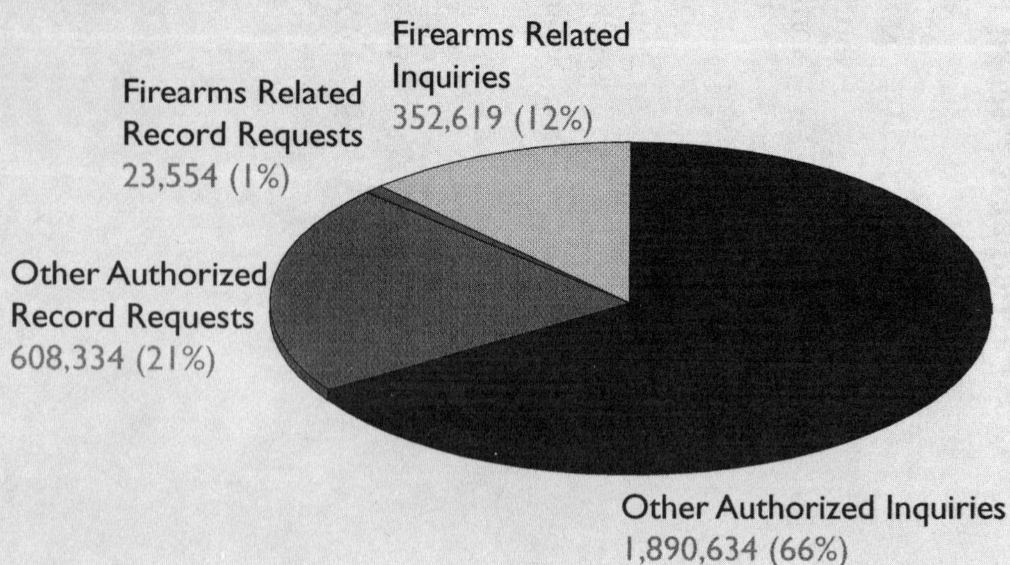

Marc KLAAS FOUNDATION for Children

December 6, 1994
Marc Klaas Testimony
Governmental Affair Hearing

America expressed outrage over the murder and kidnap of my daughter Polly. She touched the psyche of the entire country. She inspired works of art and poetry. Her beautiful face and the grace of her movement made grown men cry. Polly's tragedy also highlighted many of the inequities of our criminal justice system. She was stolen and murdered by a violent felon with an extensive criminal record who had no right being in society. In Polly's name America has expressed outrage and demanded that steps be taken to ensure the safety of all citizens.

As our technological capabilities continue to grow, our society must put more resource into the implementation of advanced data-bases that track and monitor convicted felons upon their return to society. On the evening of October 1, 1993, sheriff's deputies had Polly's kidnapper in their custody within two hours of her abduction. If they had known of his criminal history perhaps my daughter would still be alive. Because of that tragic circumstance, and the hard work of dedicated citizens, legislators, and law enforcement officials, California now has a state of the art computer system that will provide exactly that protection.

4773 Sonoma Hwy., Box 85 - Santa Rosa, CA 95409 - Tel:(707) 537-1154 - Fax: (707) 537-0482

Marc KLAAS FOUNDATION for Children

December 6, 1994
Marc Klaas Testimony
Governmental Affair Hearing
Page 2

California's Violent Crime Information, Investigation, and Technology Act of 1994, offers local law enforcement the most potent information resource ever developed to assist in the identification, tracking, apprehension, and prosecution of habitual sexual offenders and repeat violent felons. *The Violent Crime Information Network*, within the Department of Justice enables crime analysts to electronically share their data, analysis, and findings on violent crime cases with law enforcement. *The Violent Crime Information System*, tracks and monitors violent offenders and their activities. *The Sexual Habitual Offender Program*, profiles and tracks the most serious sexual predators and assists local law enforcement in solving open cases. *The CAL-DNA Offender File*, allows local law enforcement to match DNA samples of all known sexual and violent offenders with samples taken from unsolved crimes.

These efforts should be replicated in every state, and that information should be instantaneously accessible through the *Interstate Identification Index (III)*. It is as valid for a law enforcement official in Wisconsin to have the same information available as his counterpart in California. Eighty percent of the violent crimes in America are committed by eight percent of the violent felons. One third of the felons who commit violent crimes are transients who roam the country at will. When a previously convicted felon crosses state lines they effectively erase their criminal history. Law enforcement and other agencies involved in the criminal justice system cannot determine with certainty the complete criminal history of a suspect without the resources necessary to perform the task. Therefore, they are unable to make decisions that adequately protect the public.

4773 Sonoma Hwy., Box 85 - Santa Rosa, CA 95409 - Tel:(707) 537-1154 - Fax: (707) 537-0482

Marc KLAAS FOUNDATION for Children

December 6, 1994
Marc Klaas Testimony
Governmental Affair Hearing
Page 3

States are required by federal law (42 U.S.C. 3759) to spend at least five percent of their Byrne Formula Grant money to improve their criminal justice record systems. The *Brady Bill* authorizes $100 million dollars to be distributed within a six year period to computerize state criminal records and ultimately implement an instant check system. It is the fundamental duty of government at all levels to protect the welfare and lives of innocent citizens. By demanding that our public officials invest the funds, the effort and time necessary to provide the advanced computer systems, including the (III), we can give law enforcement the tools necessary to safeguard both themselves and those they were hired to protect.

It is our priorities that are off line. The painful truth is that junk yard computer automation is more sophisticated than most states violent crime tracking systems. It is pretty pathetic that junk yards have better information systems than state government's responsible for providing for the public safety. As we approach the twenty-first century, we deserve a law enforcement capability that utilizes the advanced technology available in the waning years of the twentieth century. We must demand that the world that our children inherit from us is safer than the one we inherited from our parents.

4773 Sonoma Hwy., Box 85 - Santa Rosa, CA 95409 - Tel:(707) 537-1154 - Fax: (707) 537-0482

THE SEXUAL PREDATOR ACT OF 1994

SBX 12 (Thompson, Presley, Lockyer)

Chaptered July 7, 1994

- Funds an automated supervised release file to track parolees who may be prone to violent offenses or sex crimes.

- Funds a statewide Sexual Habitual Offender Program (SHOP) Task Force composed of Department of Justice Special Agents to monitor repeat serious sex offenders.

- Creates the Violent Crime Information Network to enable the Department of Justice to electronically share information with law enforcement agencies on child abuse, missing persons, child abductions, and sexual assaults to assist in identifying, tracking and apprehending violent offenders.

- Expands the Violent Crime Information System (VCIS) to compare unsolved crime scene information against a file of known violent sexual assault, kidnapping, and homicide offenders. VCIS will provide local law enforcement with some 900 investigative leads annually to solve violent crimes. The system will house the records of more than 40,000 sexual/violent habitual offenders.

- Expands DOJ's SHOP to provide law enforcement with some 4,000 investigative leads annually. Moves up the effective date for statewide expansion of SHOP by 24 months (to June 30, 1995).

- Updates California's sex offender registration system by tracking down correct addresses of registrants. Estimates indicate that 76% of the 65,000 current registrant addresses are inaccurate.

- Expands the Cal-DNA Offender Identification Data Bank to meet increased workload that will result from expansion of SHOP and complete backlog of matching 18,900 samples from convicted sex offenders. With this expansion, the DNA laboratory will be able to complete the Sex Offender DNA Identification data bank by January, 1997, 18 months earlier than expected.

Display 1993-1994 Bill Text - INFORMATION
BILL NUMBER: SBX1 12

BILL TEXT

CHAPTER	6
FILED WITH SECRETARY OF STATE	JULY 7, 1994
APPROVED BY GOVERNOR	JULY 7, 1994
PASSED THE SENATE	JULY 7, 1994
PASSED THE ASSEMBLY	JULY 7, 1994
AMENDED IN ASSEMBLY	MAY 17, 1994
AMENDED IN SENATE	MARCH 23, 1994
AMENDED IN SENATE	MARCH 8, 1994
AMENDED IN SENATE	FEBRUARY 23, 1994
AMENDED IN SENATE	FEBRUARY 15, 1994
AMENDED IN SENATE	FEBRUARY 1, 1994
AMENDED IN SENATE	JANUARY 12, 1994

INTRODUCED BY Senators Thompson, Dills, Hayden, Hughes, Marks, McCorquodale, and Watson
(Principal coauthor: Senator Presley)
(Coauthors: Senators Ayala, Calderon, and Lockyer)
(Principal coauthors: Assembly Members Areias, Burton, and Umberg)
(Coauthors: Assembly Members Alpert, Bornstein, Bronshvag, Valerie Brown, Conroy, Costa, Gotch, Hauser, Honeycutt, Katz, Martinez, Moore, O'Connell, Rainey, and Snyder)

JANUARY 5, 1994

An act to amend Section 14200 of, and to add Sections 13885.1, 14201.1, and 14202.1 to, the Penal Code, relating to crimes, making an appropriation therefor, and declaring the urgency thereof, to take effect immediately.

LEGISLATIVE COUNSEL'S DIGEST

SB 12, Thompson. Crimes: violent and sex offenders.

(1) Existing law provides for the Serious Habitual Offender Program (SHOP) under which the Department of Justice is required to establish and maintain a comprehensive file of certain existing information regarding persons identified as sexual habitual offenders, as defined. The Department of Justice is required to provide summary profiles and complete files of information on sexual habitual offenders to law enforcement agencies, as specified.

BILL TEXT

(2) Existing law also requires the department to accept and maintain specified registration information regarding persons required to register upon conviction of certain sex offenses.

(3) Existing law also requires the department to do certain acts related to facilitating the analysis of DNA and other genetic typing analysis at its DNA laboratory, filing and maintaining this information in an offender's file or computerized data bank system, and releasing the information to law enforcement agencies and district attorneys' offices, as specified.

This bill would require the Attorney General to establish and maintain a statewide Sexual Habitual Offender Program special force, a Violent Crime Information System, and a Violent Crime Information Network.

This bill would appropriate $7,931,225 from the General Fund to the Department of Justice for expenditure during the 1994-95 fiscal year for specified purposes as follows:

(a) The sum of $739,082 for support of the Violent Crime Information Network (VCIN).

(b) The sum of $838,893 for implementing and supporting the Violent Crime Information System (VCIS).

(c) The sum of $850,000 for the addition of the Supervised Release File to the California Law Enforcement Telecommunications System (CLETS).

(d) The sum of $536,698 to support the expansion of SHOP described in (1) above.

(e) The sum of $1,179,171 to update and enhance the sex offender registration system described in (2) above.

(f) The sum of $1,999,411 for the expansion and support of the DNA files and bank described in (3) above which shall contain certain profiles of sex and violent offenders and profiles of evidence in unsolved sexual crimes.

(g) The sum of $1,787,970 to support a statewide Sexual Habitual Offender Program special force.

(4) The bill would declare that it is to take effect immediately as an urgency statute.

Appropriation: yes.

THE PEOPLE OF THE STATE OF CALIFORNIA DO ENACT AS FOLLOWS:

SECTION 1. This act shall be known and may be cited as the "Thompson-Presley Violent Crime Information, Investigation, and Technology Act of 1994."

SEC. 2. Section 13885.1 is added to the Penal Code, to read:

13885.1. The Attorney General shall establish and maintain, upon appropriation of funds by the Legislature, a statewide Sexual Habitual Offender Program special force. The special force shall be comprised of three special agent teams, one team each from southern, central, and northern California. The teams shall focus on repeat sex offenders, and perform the following activities:

(a) Coordinate state and local investigative resources to apprehend sexual habitual offenders and persons required to register under Section 290 who violate the law or conditions of probation or parole.

(b) Target and monitor chronic repeat violent sex offenders before the commission of additional sexual offenses.

(c) Develop profiles in unsolved sexual assault cases.

SEC. 3. Section 14200 of the Penal Code is amended to read:

14200. The Attorney General shall establish and maintain the Violent Crime Information Center to assist in the identification and the apprehension of persons responsible for specific violent crimes and for the disappearance and exploitation of persons, particularly children and dependent adults. The center shall establish and maintain programs which include, but are not limited to, all of the following: developing violent offender profiles; assisting local law enforcement agencies and county district attorneys by providing investigative information on persons responsible for specific violent crimes and missing person cases; providing physical description information and photographs, if available, of missing persons to county district attorneys, nonprofit missing persons organizations, and schools; and providing statistics on missing dependent adults and on missing children, including, as may be applicable, family abductions, nonfamily abductions, voluntary missing, and lost children or lost dependent adults.

SEC. 4. Section 14201.1 is added to the Penal Code, to read:

14201.1. The Attorney General shall establish and maintain, upon appropriation of funds by the Legislature, the Violent Crime Information Network within the center to enable the Department of Justice crime analysts with expertise in child abuse, missing persons, child abductions, and sexual assaults to electronically share their data, analysis, and findings on violent crime cases with each other, and to electronically provide law enforcement agencies with information to assist in the identification, tracking, and apprehension of violent offenders. The Violent Crime Information Network shall serve to integrate existing state, federal, and civilian data bases into a single comprehensive network.

SEC. 5. Section 14202.1 is added to the Penal Code, to read:

14202.1. The Attorney General shall establish and maintain, upon appropriation of funds by the Legislature, within the center the Violent Crime Information System to track and monitor violent offenders and their activities. The Violent Crime Information System shall use computer technology to compare unsolved crime scene and methods of operation information against the file of known violent sexual assault, kidnapping, and homicide offenders, containing over 40,000 violent, kidnapping, and homicide offenders. The system shall provide local law enforcement agencies with investigative leads to assist in the resolution of violent crimes.

BILL TEXT

SEC. 6. The sum of seven million nine hundred thirty-one thousand two hundred twenty-five dollars ($7,931,225) is hereby appropriated from the General Fund to the Department of Justice for expenditure during the 1994-95 fiscal year in the following amounts for the following purposes:

(a) The sum of seven hundred thirty-nine thousand eighty-two dollars ($739,082) for the support of the Violent Crime Information Network (VCIN) created pursuant to Section 14201.1 of the Penal Code.

(b) The sum of eight hundred thirty-eight thousand eight hundred ninety-three dollars ($838,893) for the implementation and support of the Violent Crime Information System created pursuant to Section 14202.1 of the Penal Code.

(c) The sum of eight hundred fifty thousand dollars ($850,000) for the addition of the Supervised Release File to the California Law Enforcement Telecommunications System (CLETS). The 24-hour computerized file shall alert law enforcement officers conducting routine traffic stops that the individual inquired upon is a registered sex or arson offender, is on active parole or probation, including any conditions of parole that may apply, or is considered a career criminal. The file shall also provide a history of law enforcement field contacts with the persons contained in the file.

(d) The sum of five hundred thirty-six thousand six hundred ninety-eight dollars ($536,698) to support the expansion of the Sexual Habitual Offender Program, created pursuant to Section 13885.2 of the Penal Code, in order to assist law enforcement agencies in the investigation of sexually motivated crimes by monitoring and tracking the most violent and repeat offenders.

(e) The sum of one million one hundred seventy-nine thousand one hundred seventy-one dollars ($1,179,171) to update and enhance the sexual offender registration system described in Section 290 of the Penal Code.

(f) The sum of one million nine hundred ninety-nine thousand four hundred eleven dollars ($1,999,411) for the expansion and support of the DNA offender file or computerized data bank system maintained pursuant to Section 290.2 of the Penal Code. The file or bank shall contain DNA profiles from convicted sex offenders and other violent predators and DNA profiles of evidence in unsolved sexual crimes consistent with Section 290.2 of the Penal Code. Law enforcement DNA laboratories locally and in other states shall access the file or bank to match archived DNA profiles with DNA samples from unsolved crimes in conformity with Section 290.2 of the Penal Code.

(g) The sum of one million seven hundred eighty-seven thousand nine hundred seventy dollars ($1,787,970) to support a statewide Sexual Habitual Offender Program special force created pursuant to Section 13885.1 of the Penal Code.

SEC. 7. This act is an urgency statute necessary for the immediate preservation of the public peace, health, or safety within the meaning of Article IV of the Constitution and shall go into immediate effect. The facts constituting the necessity are:

In order to provide necessary funding for the Violent Crime Information Network, the Violent Crime Information System, and the California Law Enforcement Telecommunications System at the beginning of the 1994-95 fiscal year, it is necessary that this act take effect immediately.

OFFICE OF THE SHERIFF
CONSOLIDATED CITY OF JACKSONVILLE

501 EAST BAY STREET • JACKSONVILLE, FLORIDA 32202-2975

JAMES E. McMILLAN
Sheriff

STATEMENT

OF

W.C.BROWN

DIRECTOR OF OPERATIONS

OFFICE OF THE SHERIFF

JACKSONVILLE, FLORIDA

DECEMBER 6, 1994

BEFORE THE

COMMITTEE ON GOVERNMENTAL AFFAIRS

UNITED STATES SENATE

I would like to begin by asking the committee, distinguished guests, and the audience if any of the following names sound familiar? Doyle White, Timothy Whitfield, Harvey Lucas, Chris Hagen. They probably don't "ring a bell". Now, let's try it again---same people, same order: Gerald Delane Murray, Gary Ray Bowles, Henry Lee Lucas, Ted Bundy. For those of you who still don't know who I am talking about, you, above all, will appreciate the dilemma of a police officer---by himself, under ordinary circumstances, in an ordinary city, doing his job like any other policeman in public service, dealing with the millions of ordinary people who work, play, drive, and walk the streets of our great nation. Would it surprise you that each of these men, given the vastness of this great land, walked our streets among our citizens, and at some point, came to the attention of a Jacksonville Sheriff's Office policeman?

If you put a pin in a map of this nation, everywhere there was a victim of each of these killers, and draw a line following the thousands of miles of highways and roadways, cutting through the cities, towns, and villages, each of these men passed, imagine the tens of thousands of citizens and children they had to have passed, each a potential victim. Then, you begin to realize how it is these men touched the lives of so many. All of this is after the first victim, and before the suspects' positive identification, or trial, or media attention that makes their names household words.

As a twenty-five year veteran of police work, I must ask myself; how many times did these serial killers come to the attention of local, state, and federal police officers? Of even more interest, is how many officers had circumstance enough or felt suspicious enough to do a formal name check? My street experience tells me that depending on the degree of difficulty, or confidence in what few systems we have, there were many more informal contacts than those we have official record of.

Our most recent example, Gary Ray Bowles, alias Timothy Ronald Whitfield was living somewhere in Jacksonville Beach and was working out of Ameri-Force Labor Pool, also located in Jacksonville Beach. Bowles was picked up under the name of Timothy Whitfield on November 22, 1994 by Jacksonville Beach Police and was transported to the Jacksonville Sheriff's Office, Homicide Unit. During the Interview it was learned that Whitfield was, in fact, Gary Ray Bowles. Bowles confessed to six (6) murders, including the one that occurred in Jacksonville. At the time of the arrest, there were three (3) outstanding warrants from other jurisdictions.

- **Warrants for Outstanding Murder:** Montgomery County, Maryland, Savannah, Georgia, Nassau County, and Florida
- Birth Certificate and Social Security Card taken from murder scene, and was used to obtain a Florida Driver's License under the name of "Timothy Ronald Whitfield".
- Gary Ray Bowles was either arrested or known to use fifteen (15) different alias' throughout the country.
- He was arrested in Jacksonville Beach on November 12, 1994, for a minor misdemeanor offense under the alias name of "Timothy Whitfield".
- He was arrested throughout the country under the name of Gary Ray Bowles numerous times from 1982 through 1993.
- He was arrested in St. Johns County, Florida on September 24, 1994, on an outstanding capias for a minor misdemeanor offense.

The problem is seen at its worst in the tracking and identifying repeat violent offenders and serial killers. But of possibly more concern to citizen and officer safety are people like Matthew K. Brown and Tony Wilson. Matthew K. Brown, AKA Keith Kelvin, Jamaican Posse Gang member, killed one of our police officers, and wounded another. Tony Wilson, AKA "Roadblock", was leader of the Outlaw Motorcycle Gang and a murderer. Given the growth in this nation of criminal gangs, hate groups, and subversive groups; the ability of officers to do computer checks quickly, reliably, and with minimal confusion is a matter of life and death for both the officer and the citizen who could be the next victim.

Of special focus by the committee is the issue of rapists and child molesters who move from job to job, city to city, remaining invisible and anonymous. This issue is of extreme concern where individuals blend into the fabric of our communities and "fit right in", working with our most vulnerable citizens in some of our most sensitive institutions such as daycare centers, schools, and hospitals.

Accordingly, I strongly recommend the continued development of any applied technologies that will assist police agencies to share information and contribute to information systems, not just locally or regionally, but at the state and national levels. This should include consideration of centers for automated fingerprints, photographs and the ability to identify the use alias and forgery to deceive officials. Special attention should be given to the identification of repeat violent offenders, serial killers, rapists, child molesters, and where they exist, possible gang and subversive group members.

I would like to close by thanking the committee for the time and opportunity to share our concerns for not just police safety, but that of the citizens and children who fall victim at the hands of people who we fail, can not, or do not have the means to identify. In so many cases, it is preventable if only there were the means.

SEARCH
The National Consortium for Justice Information and Statistics

Dr. Francis J. Carney Jr.
Chairman

Gary R. Cooper
Executive Director

**THE HONORABLE BYRON L. DORGAN,
CHAIRMAN**

**GOVERNMENT WASTE PROJECT
COMMITTEE ON GOVERNMENT AFFAIRS
UNITED STATES SENATE**

DECEMBER 6, 1994

INTRODUCTION

Mr. Chairman. I am James V. Martin, a Major and Assistant Director of the South Carolina Law Enforcement Division, where I am responsible for the criminal justice information and communications system. I appear here today as South Carolina's governor's appointee to and a representative of SEARCH, the National Consortium for Justice Information and Statistics, on which I am a member of the Board of Directors and serve as Chairman of the SEARCH Law and Policy Committee.

SEARCH is a non-profit criminal justice organization, chartered by state criminal justice officials, supported by state dues, and governed by an assembly of governor appointees from each of the fifty states, the District of Columbia, Puerto Rico and the Virgin Islands. For a quarter of a century, SEARCH's mission has been to assist state and local criminal justice agencies in the use of computers and information technology to combat crime, including the development of effective national and state law and policy in this area.

SEARCH's voice has been especially strong in supporting the creation and full implementation of the Interstate Identification Index or III. The continued success of this decentralized, national system for the interstate exchange of criminal history record information is critical to the nation's ability to deliver high quality criminal history record information in a

7311 Greenhaven Drive, Suite 145 • Sacramento, California 95831
Telephone (916) 392-2550 • Facsimile (916) 392-8440

cost-effective and timely way for a wide range of critical criminal justice and, increasingly, noncriminal justice uses. In light of SEARCH's active commitment to III, we are delighted to be asked to testify and we applaud your interest and leadership, and your staff's fine work.

I also want to recognize and credit the extraordinary work of the FBI in adopting the III concept and working actively and effectively for its full implementation. Finally, on behalf of SEARCH, I want to recognize and applaud the indispensable contribution to the III made by the FBI's Advisory Policy Board (APB). The APB is comprised of state and local criminal justice officials and provides a vital link between the FBI and state and local criminal justice information community. I am proud to say, not only as a member of SEARCH but as a member of the APB and their Subcommittee on the Revitalization and the Automation of the FBI's National Identification Division, that the APB has been a catalyst and a leader in developing and supporting the III.

The criminal justice information community has come a long way in building the III but we have a long way to go, and thus this hearing and the Congress' interest and support is critical. I want to take a few minutes and review the development of the III; its current status; and the challenges that lie ahead for III if it is to meet its full potential.

WHY AND HOW WAS THE INTERSTATE IDENTIFICATION INDEX ESTABLISHED?

Those of us in the criminal justice information community sometimes overlook a threshold but entirely appropriate question -- why does the nation need a system for the automated, interstate exchange of criminal history record information.

Simply stated, we need a national system for the interstate exchange of criminal history record information because most people arrested for criminal offenses have prior arrest records and many of them have arrest records in more than one state. Federal Bureau of Investigation officials have estimated that of all federal and state arrest fingerprint cards processed by the FBI, which includes submissions for most of the arrests in the country for serious offenses, two-thirds of the arrest subjects have prior arrests. Further, of the criminal subjects in the FBI's automated files of state and federal offenders, an estimated 25 to 30 percent are "multistate" offenders; that is, they have both federal and state records or arrests in more than one state.

Obviously, then, there is a need for some efficient means of performing a national criminal record search other than the impractical approach of making separate queries to all of the other states and jurisdictions that operate central criminal history repositories.

Prior to 1971, the only means of obtaining such a national search was by application to the FBI, which, under congressional authorization dating back to 1924, maintains criminal record files containing fingerprints and arrest and disposition information pertaining to federal and state offenders. Most search applications were handled by mail and required manual processing by FBI personnel.

In 1971, the FBI's National Crime Information Center (NCIC) implemented an on-line interstate computerized system called the Computerized Criminal History (CCH) Program. Like the FBI manual system, CCH was a "national repository" system; that is, full criminal history records for federal offenders and state offenders from participating states were maintained in the FBI's centralized database. The CCH system continued throughout the 1970s even though participation by the states was poor, due primarily to objections to the cost and difficulty of maintaining duplicate files on state offenders at both the state and federal levels.

Most state officials and SEARCH preferred the development of a "decentralized" national criminal history record system; that is, a system that would not entail the continuance of a duplicative FBI repository of criminal records, but instead would undertake to strengthen the state repositories and provide the means of tying them together, through the FBI, into a viable interstate system.

Recognizing this progress, in 1978 the U.S. Department of Justice, state officials, the FBI, SEARCH and the Advisory Policy Board all supported the concept of the Interstate Identification Index. The FBI and selected states began testing and implementation of the concept in 1980.

Growing out of this background, III was created to serve several critical objectives.

- To promote federalism through decentralization of the national criminal history record system.
- To promote cost efficiency by avoiding the cost for the states of sending all records to the FBI and avoiding the cost for the FBI of maintaining a redundant criminal history record system at the federal level.
- To promote accuracy and completeness by keeping the records "at home" and holding state central repositories responsible for obtaining dispositions and otherwise maintaining the accuracy and completeness of the criminal history record information.
- To promote appropriate and responsible criminal history record information use by both the criminal justice and authorized noncriminal justice requestors by creating a system that can deliver complete criminal history record information on a reliable and timely basis.

CURRENT STATUS OF III

When III is fully implemented, the FBI will no longer maintain duplicate criminal history files for state offenders. Rather, the FBI will maintain:

- Federal offender records, containing arrest and disposition information pertaining to persons arrested for federal offenses;
- The Interstate Identification Index itself, containing names and identifying information for all state and federal offenders in the system; and
- The National Fingerprint File (NFF), containing fingerprints of federal offenders and a single set of fingerprints for each indexed state offender from each state in which the person has been arrested.

The Interstate Identification Index and the National Fingerprint File provide the means of conducting national criminal record searches (both name searches and fingerprint-based searches) and "pointing" the inquiring agency to the FBI and/or any participating state repository that maintains a criminal record on the subject.. Inquiring agencies are then able to obtain the records directly from the indicated state or federal files by means of the NCIC telecommunications network or the National Law Enforcement Telecommunications System (NLETS), a system maintained by the states.

It is important to emphasize that the III system, when fully implemented, will be a decentralized system that will supplant the FBI's recordkeeping responsibility for state offenders by making the state repositories primarily responsible for record maintenance and dissemination. State agencies will no longer submit fingerprint cards and disposition information to the FBI for all criterion arrests, as they now do. Rather, they will channel fingerprints through their state repositories and the repositories will submit only "first-arrest" fingerprint cards to the FBI for inclusion in the NFF and for updating III. State repositories will not send "second and subsequent" arrest fingerprints to the FBI, nor will charge or disposition information for any arrests be sent. Thus, the state repositories will become the only sources of state criminal history records for these arrests -- for both criminal justice and noncriminal justice purposes.

The III system has been partially implemented through a series of tests and operational phases that began in 1980. At present, except for national security purposes and certain weapons licensing purposes and general noncriminal justice testing in Florida, North Carolina and Oregon, the system is utilized for criminal justice purposes only.

As of December, 1994, 29 state repositories are participating in the III system as direct record providers, which means that they are responding to criminal justice requests for their III-indexed records from local, state and federal criminal justice agencies nationwide. The group includes repositories in all of the largest population states. Numerous other state repositories plan to begin participating as record providers within the next few years and all states have plans for their repositories to join III at some future time. In the meantime, the FBI continues to provide the records of nonparticipating states, as described earlier, and to provide some older state records that participating states have not automated.

At present the III system provides access to in excess of 21,182,040 automated records. Of these, 11,801,279 records are maintained by the participating state repositories and 9,380,761 are maintained by the FBI. Over 1,756,000 inquiry transactions are processed each month. These inquiries are for criminal justice purposes, including criminal investigations. On the average, a positive response is provided for one out of three inquiries. Inquiry transactions are processed by the III computer within five seconds. More than 478,000 criminal histories are provided monthly through the III system. Because the III system is not being used for handling interstate noncriminal justice requests, except on a limited test basis, such requests continue to be handled by the FBI. For this reason, the FBI's files of state offenders must continue to be maintained and must be kept up-to-date.

CHALLENGES FOR III

The III is no longer merely an attractive concept. III has proven itself to be a successful and effective, operational system for the delivery of criminal history record information for criminal justice purposes. Nonetheless, key challenges lie ahead and much work remains to be done.

Noncriminal Justice Use

Perhaps the most critical challenge is to develop the III for noncriminal justice purposes. Only when the III is available for noncriminal justice use will it be possible to decentralize the national criminal history system. As long as III is off-limits to noncriminal justice users, these users must rely upon the FBI and this means that the FBI must maintain a complete criminal history system.

In order to use III for noncriminal justice purposes, most states will have to make changes in their laws and policies governing the dissemination of criminal history records. While all states permit virtually unrestricted access to all types of criminal history records for criminal justice purposes, state laws and policies governing access and use for noncriminal justice purposes are extremely diverse, ranging from essentially "open record" access in a few states to very restrictive access rules in a few states, especially concerning records of arrests without recorded dispositions or records of cases that resulted in favorable outcomes for the accused person. The other states fall somewhere in between, with sometimes complex statutory and regulatory approaches that differ greatly as to the types of noncriminal justice agencies that may have access to particular types of records for particular purposes.

For these reasons, the III system concept proposes a uniform standard for interstate noncriminal justice access and dissemination with which all participating state repositories would comply and would provide full criminal history record information in response to out-of-state record requests for:

- Criminal justice purposes;
- Noncriminal justice purposes authorized by federal laws and regulations -- primarily federal agency employment, national security purposes, military recruiting, and employment in the banking and securities/commodities industries; and
- Noncriminal justice purposes authorized by approved state statutes -- primarily state governmental licensing and employment.

States would continue to enforce their own dissemination laws governing the availability of criminal history records to nonfederal agencies located within their state borders. However, access requests by federal agencies and out-of-state agencies would be governed by the uniform III access rules outlined above.

A pilot project to test the use of the III system for handling noncriminal justice requests is currently being undertaken by the FBI and the state repositories in Florida, North Carolina and

Oregon. Since the laws of these states permit record service to all current FBI users, their repositories were able to undertake an obligation to provide record responses for all in-state and out-of-state requests. These states are submitting only the first-arrest fingerprints to the FBI and are not submitting any disposition information. The test in Florida began on April 21, 1991 and evaluation of the progress of the test has been favorable. The test in North Carolina began on February 15, 1993, in order to more fully assess III concept requirements. Oregon began participating in the test in the spring of 1994. For these states, and in a very real sense for the whole nation, III has now gone "beyond the point of no return". If III were abandoned, the FBI could no longer act as a surrogate for these three states for arrests occurring during the test period.

Interstate Compact

When decentralization is accomplished and state criminal justice agencies cease submitting charge and disposition information to the FBI, the FBI's files of state offenders will be essentially eliminated. The participating state repositories will become the only sources of complete and up-to-date information on state offenders. Thus, legal protections must be in place to ensure that the states will continue to make appropriate information available to authorized noncriminal justice users in other states and to authorized federal agencies. In addition, there is a need for the establishment of a policymaking council to provide policy direction for the use of the III system for noncriminal justice purposes.

Although these goals could possibly be realized through the enactment of federal legislation, uniform state laws or independent state legislative action, there has been a strong consensus, almost since the emergence of the III concept, that favors the use of an interstate/federal-state compact to implement the system.

The primary advantages of a compact are as follows:

- It must be ratified in identical form by all parties and, after ratification, no party can unilaterally amend it.

- Ratifying parties can withdraw from the compact only through the same formal action used for ratification, a feature that provides some assurance of long-term participation by ratifying parties.
- Since compacts take precedence over conflicting state or federal laws and since the compact authorizes the state repositories to provide record responses for all authorized III purposes, ratification of the compact would have the effect of providing the repositories with needed interstate record dissemination authority in those cases where such authority is now lacking under state law.

Work on a compact to implement the III system has been underway for over five years, with input from federal and state officials and from numerous organizations representing state and federal interests. The FBI Director has approved the compact as has the Attorney General.

The compact is currently at OMB and it is our hope that it will be sent to the Congress early in 1995. The compact must be presented to the Congress for approval in order to authorize federal (FBI) participation and the Congress must formally consent to entry into the compact by the states, since the compact deals with subjects of federal interest. Mr. Chairman, we hope that the compact will have your leadership and support. Ratification action in some state legislatures could begin during 1995. Ratification of the compact has not yet been made a condition of state participation in III, but it is expected that all participating states will ratify the compact since, in most states, it will provide record dissemination authority now lacking under state laws.

Implementation

The III faces other challenges. One such challenge, of course, is that the remaining states must as quickly as possible be brought into III participation. This requires not just good intentions, but the technical capacity to respond to authorized searches on an on-line basis. State efforts to participate in III involve acquiring the necessary system capacity to be able to interface with III and handle the workload and developing some required procedures to ensure system security and maintain record quality. Many nonparticipating states are close to being able to join

III but others, unfortunately, are years away from having the technical infrastructure necessary to participate. In addition, some of the present III states are participating at a rather minimal level -- that is, they have not assumed responsibility for all of the offenders from their states whose records are maintained by the FBI. These states need to make additional improvements and upgrades to become full III participants.

Accuracy And Completeness

Another challenge facing the III is to continue to improve the accuracy and completeness of the nation's criminal history records. Ultimately, III is only as good as the quality of the records which the system accesses and disseminates. Incomplete disposition reporting and, to a lesser extent, incomplete arrest reporting from local agencies to state repositories is a well-documented problem. SEARCH, along with our colleagues at the FBI, in the APB and, of course, the state repositories, has made it a priority to emphasize the dimensions of this problem and campaign for implementing strategies to improve data quality.

Today, many states have developed excellent systems which are automated and which have disposition reporting rates for arrests reported in the last five years near or exceeding 90 percent. Thus, we know that high quality criminal history record systems can be built and we know how to build them. The effort requires state and federal money; technological upgrades -- in particular, on-line telecommunications connections between the courts and the state repository -- and the implementation of a mix of data quality strategies including mandatory disposition reporting requirements and delinquent disposition monitoring systems. The full implementation of III will also improve data quality by fixing responsibility for the records on the state repository and by eliminating an additional step in the reporting chain created by the requirement that states report multiple and subsequent arrests and dispositions to the FBI.

III And Brady

The Brady Act requires that no later than November, 1998 the Attorney General establish a national instant check system for the immediate and accurate identification of felons who attempt to purchase firearms. The Attorney General has identified III as the Brady instant check system. This designation is welcome in that it puts pressure on the states to upgrade their criminal history record systems; improve the quality of the records in those systems; and be fully participating in III. The Brady designation is also welcome because it provides critical federal financial resources for III participation.

There is still much to be done before November 1998 to increase the percentage of records available through III that have dispositions and felony flags, so that the III system can provide an effective national instant check system.

CONCLUSION

We are at an historic moment. In a very real sense the III is beyond the point of no return. All of us in the state and federal criminal justice information community, the Congress and the state legislatures, have to work together to achieve full III implementation and to reap the benefits of a decentralized national criminal history system. Together, we can deliver better quality records in an efficient and timely manner with respect for civil liberties and responsiveness to the needs of criminal justice and noncriminal justice users.

Congressional attention to and support for the III of the kind represented by this hearing is critical. For this reason, SEARCH applauds your leadership, Mr. Chairman, and encourages your continued attention to this important issue.

STATEMENT

OF

PATRICK J. DOYLE

SPECIAL AGENT IN CHARGE

FLORIDA DEPARTMENT OF LAW ENFORCEMENT

TALLAHASSEE, FLORIDA

DECEMBER 6, 1994

BEFORE THE

COMMITTEE ON GOVERNMENTAL AFFAIRS

UNITED STATES SENATE

Interstate Identification Index (III)

The Interstate Identification Index (III), commonly referred to as "Triple I", was implemented in 1983 as a pointer index to allow participating states to respond directly to inquiries involving their respective computerized criminal history (CCH) files. Prior to Triple I, the Federal Bureau of Investigation (FBI) maintained the CCH records for all states and responded to all inquiries concerning these records. The implementation of Triple I has provided a mechanism for participating states to exercise more control over the dissemination of their records, while resulting in virtually instantaneous availability of this information for users of the system, including investigators, prosecutors and the courts.

The Triple I system has proven to be a valuable tool for the criminal justice community. The state of Florida had the distinct honor of serving as the pilot state during the early developmental stages of III in 1980 and 1981. Since that time, the utility of Triple I has been evidenced repeatedly as illustrated by the following uses of III derived information in the state of Florida:

Investigative. Agencies are linked together to share information concerning the existence of arrest records in one state on a subject under investigation in another state. Frequently, additional identification data, photographs, current addresses, etc. are shared amongst agencies once the initial pointer establishes the availability of a record in another state. During the period January - October 1994, there were 30,084,752 inquiries and record request transactions processed through the Triple I system nationwide. In the state of Florida alone during this same period, there were 457,584 criminal fingerprint card transactions, 272,694 applicant fingerprint card transactions, 376,070 public records law transactions and 254,194 Firearms Purchase Program transactions. Over five hundred thousand criminal fingerprint cards were processed last year in Florida, with approximately 65 to 70% identified with an existing record either in Florida or elsewhere in the United States.

Prosecutorial. Decisions concerning the prosecution of an offender as an "habitual offender" are facilitated through criminal history records obtained through Triple I. Out of State convictions are counted when calculating a subject's habitual offender status.

Judicial. Past criminal acts have a direct bearing on sentencing guidelines and recommended sentences. Out of state information derived through Triple I is extremely critical in this process, frequently resulting in longer recommended sentences.

Custodial. The nature and circumstances surrounding a subject's criminal history record will have an influence on the level of security deemed appropriate for subsequent incarceration.

Employment. The utility of Triple I as a proactive, preventative measure is realized through it's use in the employment arena. Florida laws requiring a criminal history record check for day care center workers, school teachers and persons working with the elderly undoubtedly steer undesirable applicants away from these professions where they would have direct daily contact with the most vulnerable members of society. During the past year, there were 315,525 applicant fingerprint cards processed in Florida along with 404,138 requests via correspondence, for a total of 719,663 employment related criminal history record checks. Many of these inquiries are not conducted through Triple I since they are for non-criminal justice agencies/persons having access to Florida criminal history records by virtue of Florida's public records law. Since employment based record checks average a 10% ident rate (10% of the applicants are matched with existing criminal history records), almost 72,000 identifications are made annually via applicant record checks. In addition, approximately 1% of the inquiries result in a hit on an active wanted person's record, therefore, over 7,000 warrants have the potential to be served.

Firearms Purchase. During the past year, a total of 333,670 record checks were conducted under Florida's Firearms Purchase Program. Approximately 5 % of these checks were idents, and 3% (or approximately 10,000) resulted in disqualifying the individual from purchasing a handgun.

The benefits of the Triple I system as illustrated above are obvious, however, it must be understood that there are deficiencies associated with this system which must also be addressed. Of primary concern to the users of Triple I is the absence of disposition data in a large number of criminal history records. Although denouncers of Triple I may attribute this deficiency to the Triple I system itself, in reality this is a record keeping/reporting issue which would exist whether the record was requested through Triple I, manual criminal history files or any other manner. Regardless of the cause of the lack of dispositions, a solution needs to be identified and implemented to ensure the availability of complete and accurate records.

Concerted efforts to obtain final disposition data on felony arrests in Florida have resulted in a felony disposition rate of 69% and an overall disposition rate exceeding 50% for Florida arrests. Florida's efforts entailed a statutory shift of the responsibility for disposition reporting from the arresting agency to the clerk of the court, and the use of federal grant monies to obtain missing felony disposition data from previous years. Although progress has been made in Florida, there is still a considerable amount of improvement necessary.

A second problem frequently cited about the Triple I system is the perceived lack of awareness at the local level concerning it's existence and capabilities. Although many local agency personnel may not be able to enunciate what III stands for, or what it does, they are fully aware that they can obtain out of state criminal history information through their terminal. The lack of knowledge about the particulars is a training/education issue, not a Triple I deficiency. All operators utilizing a terminal capable of accessing Triple I are required by NCIC policy to have their proficiency in NCIC policies and procedures affirmed by the state control terminal agency. In many states, they undergo structured training which includes information on Triple I, followed by a test to determine the level of proficiency.

In Florida, and undoubtedly many other states, additional training on Triple I is offered at new police chief/sheriffs meetings, in minimum standards courses, at conferences and in a study guide provided to local criminal justice agencies. It would be safe to state that virtually every law enforcement officer in Florida is aware of criminal history records and the fact that they can be obtained from other states. Is it critical that they understand how? Is it critical that they understand the acronym III? Should they also be required to know on what hardware, software and baud rate the system operates? Does it matter that they don't know the mechanics of how their patrol vehicle operates as long as they can drive it safely?

A third problem associated with the Triple I system is the non participation of many states. There are still 21 states that the FBI disseminates records for along with Federal agencies, the District of Columbia, U.S. territorial possessions, and a limited number of foreign countries. The reasons for non-participation vary, including a lack of interest because there is no motivation to participate since they have access to other states records anyway. Some states are also not capable of participation because they are not automated, or no central point of jurisdiction exists to make participation possible. This lack of participation has been recognized by the National Crime Information Center Advisory Policy Board (APB) which has discussed possible solutions on several occasions, and are in the process of making a recommendation regarding this issue.

Although there are some problems regarding the Triple I system, there are solutions available to minimize them. For example, an increase in federal funding of criminal history improvement grants will enable more states to improve their disposition reporting rates. Although funding of this nature has existed over the past several years, the amounts awarded have been woefully inadequate to make a significant difference at the national level. In the state of Florida, efforts to obtain previous disposition data resulted in an approximate expense of \$3.50 per record. Since Florida has 1.6 million records indexed in III, a disposition reporting rate of 50 % would result in the need for funding in the amount of \$2,800,000 for Florida alone. Florida also recently expended \$875,000 to establish a juvenile criminal history file, without the inclusion of disposition data. In order to obtain automated disposition data for this file, it is estimated that \$12.5 million will be required by the clerks of the court, a further indication of the dire need for additional funds.

Another possible solution to consider for improving the disposition reporting rate is to ensure that the responsibility for disposition reporting within each state is firmly affixed with the most appropriate agency. This has had a significant impact in the state of Florida and the results nationwide should be similar.

Other solutions to help improve the effectiveness of Triple I include aggressive marketing of Triple I and it's benefits, and the pursuit of additional funding for states desiring to participate that lack automation. Additional money for automating clerks of the court to facilitate on-line transmission of disposition data to the state repository and ultimately to the national level are also options to consider.

Finally, an additional measure that could have a significant impact on enhancing Triple I would be the expansion of the National Fingerprint File (NFF) phase of the Triple I program. Currently, three states (Florida, North Carolina and Oregon) participate in this phase which truly decentralizes record keeping and minimizes duplication. Through NFF, only the initial arrest is submitted to the FBI to establish the pointer index, and all remaining records are solely maintained at the state repository. By virtue of the fact that the states themselves respond to record inquiries, more complete, accurate criminal history data is available in a more timely manner. For example, many offenses not acceptable for entry at the national level are available from the states themselves, as are dispositions that were not routed to the FBI. Also, since the FBI has stricter criteria for fingerprint impressions, many arrest records have been rejected by the FBI but are maintained by the individual states. These records would be available through Triple I once the initial index was established. Resources currently devoted to processing duplicate data at the national level could be re-directed to other duties, such as gathering additional disposition data from the states and marketing NFF and Triple I.

The above recommended measures will help ensure the effectiveness of the Triple I system by helping promote it's use, improving the disposition reporting rate of records accessed through Triple I, eliminating a significant amount of duplicate record keeping and providing substantial funding to accomplish these objectives. Although Triple I is not a perfect system, it is a vast improvement over previous systems. It results in a more timely response, eliminates the expense of routing many fingerprint cards to the FBI and, even though many dispositions are absent, it points to an arrest record which is the most critically needed information that must be made readily available to our law enforcement personnel. Once an arrest record has been identified, follow up contact with the originating agency or clerk of the court can produce the desired disposition data. Let us not sacrifice the safety of our precious law enforcement officers by discontinuing a valuable program because of a few minor problems and misconceptions. Let us instead, work together in a concerted effort to make this system as beneficial and effective as it can be.

O

TOTAL P.05